WESTMAR COLLEG P9-CRI-018

TRANSNATIONAL LAW

Storrs Lectures on Jurisprudence

Yale Law School

Transnational Law

by PHILIP C. JESSUP

Hamilton Fish Professor of International Law and Diplomacy,

Columbia University

New Haven

YALE UNIVERSITY PRESS

JX
3140
.J42

34
J58t

© 1956 by Yale University Press.
Printed in the United States of America by
the Printing-Office of the Yale University Press,
New Haven, Connecticut and reprinted by
The Murray Printing Company, Forge Village, Massachusetts.

First published, October, 1956
Second printing, August, 1959

All rights reserved. This book may not be
reproduced, in whole or in part, in any form
(except by reviewers for the public press),
without written permission from the publishers.
Library of Congress catalog card number: 56–11798.

50208

To L. K. J.

11714163 June 3.15

ACKNOWLEDGMENT

THIS VOLUME reproduces, without substantial change, the Storrs Lectures delivered at the Yale Law School in February 1956. The author gratefully acknowledges the privilege of presenting them originally in that series. For aid in the preparation of the lectures, the author also expresses his appreciation for a grant from the Rockefeller Foundation; for the able research assistance of Hans Blix and Guenter Weissberg; and for the further assistance of Miss Barbara Demarest in preliminary and final work on the manuscript.

PHILIP C. JESSUP

March 15, 1956

CONTENTS

I. THE UNIVERSALITY
OF THE HUMAN PROBLEMS

T HE SUBJECT to which these chapters are addressed is the
law applicable to the complex interrelated world community which may be described as beginning with the individual and reaching on up to the so-called "family of nations" or "society of states." Human society in its development since the end of the feudal period has placed special
emphasis on the national state, and we have not yet reached
the stage of a world state. These facts must be taken into
account, but the state, in whatever form, is not the only
group with which we are concerned. The problems to be
examined are in large part those which are usually called
international, and the law to be examined consists of the
rules applicable to these problems. But the term "international" is misleading since it suggests that one is concerned
only with the relations of one nation (or state) to other
nations (or states).

Part of the difficulty in analyzing the problems of the
world community and the law regulating them is the lack
of an appropriate word or term for the rules we are discussing. Just as the word "international" is inadequate to describe the problem, so the term "international law" will not
do. Georges Scelle seeks to meet the difficulty by using the
term *droit des gens,* "not taken exclusively in its Latin ety-
mology, which still implies the notion of a collectivity, but

in its common and current meaning of *individuals,* considered simply as such and collectively as members of political societies."[1] I find no satisfactory English equivalent along these lines. Professor Alf Ross of the University of Copenhagen, speaking of the term "private international law," has wisely said: "Normally it is both hopeless and inadvisable to try to alter a generally accepted terminology, but in this case linguistic usage is so misleading that it seems to me right to make the attempt."[2] Ross's own experiment in word-coining —"interlegal law" for "private international law"—is not encouraging to me. My choice of terminology will no doubt be equally unsatisfactory to others. Nevertheless I shall use, instead of "international law," the term "transnational law" to include all law which regulates actions or events that transcend national frontiers. Both public and private international law are included, as are other rules which do not wholly fit into such standard categories.[3]

1. Georges Scelle, *Précis de droit des gens* (Paris, Recueil Sirey, 1932), pt. 1, p. vii.

2. Alf Ross, *A Textbook of International Law* (London, Longmans, Green, 1947), p. 73.

3. Myres McDougal has familiarized us with the use of the adjective "transnational" to describe groups whose composition or activities transcend national frontiers, but he does not apply the term to law in the sense in which it is used here. Joseph E. Johnson suggested more broadly the utility of the word "transnational" in place of "international" in his address of June 15, 1955, at the annual meeting of the Harvard Foundation and Law School Alumni. Occasional use of the word has also been made by Percy Elwood Corbett, *The Study of International Law* (Garden City, N.Y., Doubleday, 1955), p. 50, and by Arthur Nussbaum, *A Concise History of the Law of Nations* (rev. ed., New York, Macmillan, 1954).

The concept is similar to but not identical with Scelle's monistic theory of *un Droit intersocial unifié*.[4] One is dealing, as he says, with "human relationships transcending the limits of the various states."[5] But while I agree with him that states are not the only subjects of international law,[6] I do not go to the other extreme and say with Scelle that individuals are the only subjects. Corporate bodies, whether political or nonpolitical, have certainly been treated in orthodox theory as fictions, but their essential reality as entities is now well accepted and law deals with them as such.[7] Scelle agrees that states have characteristic features distinguishing them from other organizations, but for him these features are not of a legal order but *historico-politique*,[8] a distinction which is not drawn here.

Transnational situations, then, may involve individuals, corporations, states, organizations of states, or other groups. A private American citizen, or a stateless person for that matter, whose passport or other travel document is challenged at a European frontier confronts a transnational situation. So does an American oil company doing business in Venezuela; or the New York lawyer who retains French

4. Scelle, pp. 32ff.

5. *Ibid.*, p. 51, as paraphrased by Walter Schiffer, *The Legal Community of Mankind* (New York, Columbia University Press, 1954), p. 259.

6. Having argued in 1948 that this was a desirable position (*A Modern Law of Nations*, New York, Macmillan, 1948, ch. 2), I am prepared to say it is now established.

7. Henry E. Foley, "Incorporation, Multiple Incorporation, and the Conflict of Laws," 42 *Harvard Law Review* 516, 517–19 (1929).

8. Scelle, p. 83.

counsel to advise on the settlement of his client's estate in France; or the United States Government when negotiating with the Soviet Union regarding the unification of Germany. So does the United Nations when shipping milk for UNICEF or sending a mediator to Palestine. Equally one could mention the International Chamber of Commerce exercising its privilege of taking part in a conference called by the Economic and Social Council of the United Nations. One is sufficiently aware of the transnational activities of individuals, corporations, and states. When one considers that there are also in existence more than 140 intergovernmental organizations and over 1,100 nongovernmental organizations commonly described as international,[9] one realizes the almost infinite variety of the transnational situations which may arise.

There are rules, or there is law, bearing upon each of these situations. There may be a number of applicable legal rules and they may conflict with each other. When this is the case still other rules may determine which law prevails. In certain types of situations we may say this is a question of "choice of law" which is to be determined by the rules of "Conflict of Laws" or "Private International Law." The choice usually referred to here is between rules of different national laws; and the choice, we assume, is to be made by a national court. In other types of situations the choice may be between a rule of national law and a rule of "Public International Law," and the choice may be made by an inter-

9. *Yearbook of International Organizations, 1954–55* (Brussels, Union of International Associations, 1954).

national tribunal or by some nonjudicial decision maker.

In Scelle's monistic conception: "When the legislator of a state, or when national jurisdictions establish rules governing conflicts of laws or conflicts of jurisdiction, they lay down *rules of international law*. . . . When a national judge delivers a judgment in a case between nationals and foreigners or between foreigners, he ceases to be a *national* judge and becomes an *international* judge."[10] Another pattern of thought insists that "the only law in force in the sovereign state is its own law" and that the state's own law determines whether in certain instances some other rule from some other jurisdiction will be applied, which is made part of its law for the purpose.[11] This does not prevent the foreign law from being treated, for purposes of proof, as a "fact."[12] Similarly, the Permanent Court of International Justice has said: "From the standpoint of International Law and the Court which is its organ, municipal laws are merely facts which express the will and constitute the activities of States, in the same manner as do legal decisions or administrative measures."[13] In the United States and in other states international law is declared to be "part of our law" and therefore

10. Scelle, p. 56.

11. See American Law Institute, *Restatement of the Law of Conflict of Laws* (St. Paul, American Law Institute Publishers, 1934), ch. 1, Topic 1, sec. 1(1) and comment on sec. 5.

12. Joseph H. Beale, *A Treatise on the Conflict of Laws* (New York, Baker, Voorhis, 1935), secs. 621.4–621.6. Cf. Arthur Nussbaum, "Proving the Law of Foreign Countries," 3 *American Journal of Comparative Law* 60 (1954).

13. Case concerning certain German interests in Polish Upper Silesia (The Merits), P.C.I.J., ser. A, no. 7 (1926), p. 19.

can be applied directly by the courts. "Foreign municipal laws must indeed be proved as facts, but it is not so with the law of nations."[14] To envisage the applicability of transnational law it is necessary to avoid thinking solely in terms of any particular forum, since it is quite possible, as we shall see, to have a tribunal which does not have as its own law either a body of national law or the corpus of international law.

A problem may also be resolved not by the application of law (although equally not in violation of law) but by a process of adjustment—an extralegal or metajuridical means. Thus certain heirs may renounce their rights in an estate, or their conflicting claims may be compromised without resort to litigation. The unification of Germany might be brought about without reference to the Potsdam Agreements by a negotiated settlement acceptable to all concerned. But the results may have legal effect and be in legal form. In other words, the solution arrived at without utilizing law may itself provide the law of the case, just as in a commercial arbitration where the arbitrators are authorized to make a fair compromise. One notes that the problem of extracting and refining oil in Iran may involve—as it has—Iranian law, English law, and public international law. Procedurally it may involve—as it has—diplomatic negotiations, proceedings in the International Court of Justice and in the Security Council, business negotiations with and among oil companies, and action in the Iranian Majlis.

14. *The Paquete Habana*, 175 U.S. 677, 700 (1900); *The Scotia*, 14 Wall. 170, 188 (1871).

Perhaps it is some innate instinct for orderliness which leads the human mind endlessly to establish and to discuss classifications and definitions and to evolve theories to justify them. In international law one may be a monist or a dualist; a positivist, a naturalist, or an eclectic. The intellectual process is essential but it involves dangers. The more wedded we become to a particular classification or definition, the more our thinking tends to become frozen and thus to have a rigidity which hampers progress toward the ever needed new solutions of problems whether old or new. Conflicts and laws are made by man. So are the theories which pronounce, for example, that international law cannot confer rights or impose duties directly on an individual because, says Theory, the individual is not a subject but an object of international law. It is not inappropriate here to invoke again the high authority of an earlier Storrs lecturer and to say with Cardozo: "Law and obedience to law are facts confirmed every day to us all in our experience of life. If the result of a definition is to make them seem to be illusions, so much the worse for the definition; we must enlarge it till it is broad enough to answer to realities."[15]

As Lord Justice Denning of the Court of Appeal has said, some lawyers find solutions for every difficulty while other lawyers find difficulties for every solution. The solution suggested here is that, for the time being at least, we avoid further classification of transnational problems and further definitions of transnational law. You will not need to be a

15. Benjamin N. Cardozo, *The Nature of the Judicial Process* (New Haven, Yale University Press, 1921), p. 127.

lawyer to find the difficulties for this solution; they will be only too apparent.

What, then, is the general problem? This planet is peopled with human beings whose lives are affected by rules. This is true whether one considers the people who live in New Haven among all the complexities and refinements of civilization or the people who live in the unimproved jungle recesses of New Guinea. *Ubi societas, ibi ius.* People form groups which we call families, clans, tribes, corporations, towns, states, international organizations, or by other names. "History is, among other things, the record of groupings of human beings which for some strange reason stay together."[16] Individual interrelationships continue, but to these are added the relationships of the individual to the groups and those among the groups themselves. As Max Radin points out: "Any one grouping cuts through and across other groupings, a fact which makes all social study so difficult."[17]

As man has developed his needs and his facilities for meeting his needs, the rules become more numerous and more complicated. History, geography, preferences, convenience, and necessity have dictated dispersion of the authority to make the rules men live by. Some rules are made by the head of the family, whether it be father or mother, such as "Wash your hands before supper." Some rules are made by

16. Adolf A. Berle, *The 20th Century Capitalist Revolution* (New York, Harcourt, Brace, 1954), p. 21.

17. Max Radin, *Law as Logic and Experience* (New Haven, Yale University Press, 1940), p. 126.

ecclesiastical authorities as in specifying times and manners of fasting. Some are made by corporations regulating their sales agencies, as recently publicized in the hearings of the Senate Judiciary Antitrust and Monopoly Subcommittee on the practices of General Motors. Other rules are made by secret societies, by towns, cities, states. Still others are made by international organizations such as the Coal and Steel Community, the International Monetary Fund, or the OEEC. Much of interest is to be learned from the study of the rules of procedure of such a body as the General Assembly of the United Nations—rules which are applied by a person clothed with official authority and which often determine conclusively the fate of a proposal to which a sovereign state attaches the greatest importance.

Nowadays it is neither novel nor heretical to call all of these rules "law." In any case, there is no law forbidding a scholar to choose his own definition—or requiring him to formulate one, for that matter. In the exercise of this scholarly freedom (and scholarly freedom needs exercise at all times lest it become atrophied) I rest for the time being on this broad description of the sense in which I speak of law in general and of transnational law in particular.

What is the role of the scholar in treating international or transnational law? Surely not to hedge himself round with the adverbial and adjectival qualifications so characteristic of the language of diplomacy; or to resort to such circumlocutions as are illustrated by Burton Marshall's story of the English diplomat who was embarrassed by casual inquiries about his father, who, as a matter of fact, had died on the gallows. The diplomat learned to frame a truthful answer to such inquiries by saying: "The old gentleman suffered a lamentable death in consequence of injuries sustained in a fall caused by the collapse of the floor of a platform during a public function in which he had an important part." If what the scholar says is not subject to criticism, it might as well be left unsaid.[18] Without disparaging the contribution of pure reason he need not take the position of Grotius, who wrote in the Prolegomena of his *De Jure Belli ac Pacis:* "If anyone thinks that I have had in view any controversies of our own times, either those that have arisen or those which can be foreseen as likely to arise, he will do me an injustice. With all truthfulness I aver that, just as mathematicians treat their figures as abstracted from bodies, so in treating law I have withdrawn my mind from every particular fact."[19] I have not tried to emulate Grotius in this respect; to the contrary, I agree with Max Radin: "It is essential that no complete detachment ever takes place."[20] "Grotius was a scholar, and his only authority was that of a scholar."[21] Yet Grotius was not ignorant of statecraft, and he and succeeding scholars have not been without their influence on developments in international

18. Cf. Myres S. McDougal, "International Law, Power, and Policy: A Contemporary Conception," The Hague Academy of International Law, 82 *Recueil des Cours* 140 (1953, I).

19. Hugo Grotius, *De Jure Belli as Pacis,* vol. *2,* translated in Publications of the Carnegie Endowment for International Peace, "The Classics of International Law" (Oxford, Clarendon Press, 1927), Bk. I, pp. 29–30.

20. Radin, p. ix.

21. Walter Schiffer, *The Legal Community of Mankind,* p. 38.

politics, despite the reaction of practical people like the judges of the High Court of Admiralty in 1778. When that court was asked to declare the length of time a prize must be held *infra praesidia* in order to divest title, it said: "Grotius might as well have laid down, for a rule, twelve hours, as twenty-four; or forty-eight, as twelve. A pedantic man in his closet dictates the law of nations; everybody quotes, and nobody minds him."[22] But who will contradict the teaching that "understanding is the beginning of wisdom" or assert that wisdom is not a useful quality in a statesman? To the understanding of transnational legal problems we may then address ourselves.

The problems in general arise from conflicts of interest or desire, real or imagined. In the customary method of the study of international relations and international law, the stress is on the state or nation factor. If the matter does not involve the government of one state in its relations with another government or other governments, the matter is said to be "domestic." By and large, the orthodox approach precluded international consideration of a problem until it at least had transnational dimensions. Allow me now the liberty of this generalization, holding in reserve such questions as human rights and the older interests based on treaties for the protection of minorities. Thus a local riot not involving aliens, or agitation by citizens for the reform of their government, was not an international question. But when a dissident group inside a state was strong enough and

22. *The Renard* (1778), 1 Eng. P.C. 17, 18; Hay and Marriott 222, 224; 165 Eng. Rep. 51, 52 (Adm.).

resorted to arms, international law began to take an interest. The group might be recognized by other governments as insurgents or belligerents. The reason for the conflict would not have changed, the parties would be essentially the same, except that one internal group had now attained a certain degree of power. If the group was crushed the concern of traditional international law again subsided, although the causes of the conflict still remained unchanged. One might conclude that all this is because international law realistically takes account of power; and if power and jurisdiction are equated, then the dissident group reaches a point where it has jurisdiction to affect persons and the property of persons who belong to another group, i.e. citizens of another state. But this is not quite true, because there are different kinds of power. Power, like love, is "a many splendored thing." "A nation's power can no longer be measured in terms of Francis Bacon's catalogue of 'walled towns, stored arsenals and armories, goodly race of horses, chariots of war, elephants, ordnance and artillery.' "[23] The Democratic party by the elections of 1954 acquired great power in the United States through the control of both Houses of Congress; but international law (though not international politics)[24] ignored the very existence of the Democratic party. On the other hand, when the Chinese Communist party in 1949 acquired by force of arms the control of the Chinese mainland, international law was ready to say here is a de facto government

23. Sol M. Linowitz, "War for Men's Minds: The Fight We Must Not Lose," 41 *American Bar Association Journal* 810 (1955).
24. Cf. McDougal, p. 238.

to which rules of international law apply. The result is of course convenient, because in the one case the Democratic party chose to operate through the organs of government already established and under President Eisenhower, while in the other case the Communist party chose to operate through its own organs and to deny even the governmental existence of Nationalist China and Generalissimo Chiang Kai-shek. Thus too, as Marek points out, if there is a truly indigenous revolution which is successful, the identity and continuity of the state do not change; whereas if the revolution is a "fake" engineered and supported from outside, the ensuing puppet government, if successful, may constitute a new state, depending on whether it lives long enough to rely on the maxim *ex factis ius oritur* prevailing over the antinomic maxim *ex iniuria ius non oritur*.[25]

The point at which one passes from the archaic domains of one branch of law to another may be traced also in transnational economic relations. The "most successful experiment in economic world government thus far achieved in the twentieth century" according to Berle[26] was the Achnacarry or "As-Is" Agreement between the heads of Standard Oil of New Jersey, Shell, and Anglo-Persian. This was a "private" or nongovernmental agreement to end and avoid economic war, but there is direct governmental interest in Anglo-Persian to the extent that the British Government

---

25. Krystyna Marek, *Identity and Continuity of States in Public International Law* (Geneva, Librairie E. Droz, 1954), pp. 64ff., 564ff.
26. *The 20th Century Capitalist Revolution*, p. 147.

owns 52.5 per cent of the voting stock.[27] In current terminology it was not an international agreement, but it was a transnational one. In the 1940's American oil companies reached an agreement for distribution of profits with the Venezuelan Government on a fifty-fifty basis;[28] this too would not be called international. According to the argument of the British Government before the International Court of Justice, the oil concession agreement of April 29, 1933, between the Anglo-Persian Oil Company and the Iranian Government had "a double character, the character of being at once a concessionary contract between the Iranian Government and the Company and a treaty between the two Governments."[29] When the same problem reached a settlement in 1954 the parties were, of the first part, the Imperial Government of Iran and the National Iranian Oil Company, and of the second part a Pennsylvania corporation, a New York corporation, a New Jersey corporation, two Delaware corporations, and a British, a Dutch, and a French corporation. Article 46 of the agreement provides: "In view of the diverse nationalities of the parties to this Agreement, it shall be governed by and interpreted and applied in accordance with principles of law common to Iran and the several nations in which the other parties to this Agreement are incorporated, and in the absence of such

27. John A. Loftus, "Middle East Oil," 2 *Middle East Journal* 17, 18 (1948).

28. See Joseph E. Pogue, *Oil in Venezuela* (Petroleum Department, Chase National Bank of the City of New York, 1949).

29. Anglo-Iranian Oil Co. case (jurisdiction), Judgment of July 22nd, 1952: I.C.J. Reports 1952, p. 93 at p. 112.

common principles, then by and in accordance with principles of law recognized by civilized nations in general, including such of those principles as may have been applied by international tribunals."[30]

In the Union of International Transport by Rail, disputes are settled by an arbitral tribunal before which no distinction is made between the governmental and nongovernmental administrations, both of which are members.[31]

Obviously there is a delicate shading between the situations to which international law traditionally applies and those to which it does not. "Lawyers," writes Sigmund Timberg, ". . . have adhered to rigidly compartmentalized national legal systems, which are unable to cope with an economic order of international dimensions."[32] The use of transnational law would supply a larger storehouse of rules on which to draw, and it would be unnecessary to worry whether public or private law applies in certain cases.[33] We may find that some of the problems that we have considered essentially international, inevitably productive of stress and conflict between governments and peoples of two different countries, are after all merely human problems which might arise at any level of human society—individual, corporate,

30. The Iranian Consortium, *Government Agreement and Related Documents* (1954), p. 71.

31. Manley O. Hudson and Louis B. Sohn, "Fifty Years of Arbitration in the Union of International Transport by Rail," 37 *American Journal of International Law* 597, 600 (1943).

32. "International Combines and National Sovereigns," 95 *University of Pennsylvania Law Review* 575, 577 (1947).

33. See pp. 84ff, 106–7 (Chapter 3 of text).

interregional, or international. In spite of the vast organizational and procedural differences between the national and the international stage, if we find there are common elements in the domestic and the international dramas, may not the greater experience with the solution of the former aid in the solution of the latter? Let us experiment with three dramas, each one in two scences.

DRAMA NO. I. IN TWO SCENES

M. *v.* F.

Scene No. 1 opens as follows:

Mary wants to separate from Frank. She was poor and inexperienced when they were married many years ago, waging a hard struggle to keep going, and he promised her a much better life with full protection and freedom from all cares and responsibilities. He was a dominant fellow too, and in her feeble condition it was hard to say no. Frank fixed up the old homestead, putting a nice coat of fresh paint on the old paneling, neon lights in the ceiling, radiant heat throughout, and all the latest chromium fixtures in the kitchen where the Dutch oven used to be. But Mary never had a say about how it should be done, and the protected life in which Frank planned every trip, every dinner party, and indeed every detail of her life, began to pall. She was full of health now and had friends of her own and thought how much pleasanter it would be if, like Bernice and Philippa, she were her own master in her own house. So she went to Reno to get a divorce.

We pass to Scene No. 2:

Morocco wants to separate from France. She was caught up in the struggle of the Great Powers, and France's offer of a protectorate seemed the best solution of her troubles, and besides France was a big powerful state and it was hard to say no. France built roads and sent her colonists and increased the production of mines and fields and performed her *mission civilisatrice*. But Morocco never had a say about how it should be done, and the protected life began to pall. She was full of vigor now and had friends and thought how much pleasanter it would be if she were master in her own house like Burma and the Philippines. So she went to the United Nations to get her independence.

DRAMA NO. 2. IN TWO SCENES
West *v.* East

Turn to our second drama, Scene No. 1:

In the 1870's and 1880's the western part of the United States lived on an agricultural and mining economy. The Westerners had no capital and no industries. The railroads which carried their products to the markets were built by eastern businessmen and bankers identified as living in New York, Boston, and Philadelphia. The mortgages on their farms, the debts they owed for purchases of machinery, and the necessities of life were owned by the same faraway rich and heartless embodiments of wealth, a class of absentee landlords, or by local merchants who seemed equally remote from their interests.

". . . the Western mind was perplexed in the extreme, and

looked eagerly about for something with which to find fault
. . ."[34] "Farmers of Illinois, Wisconsin, and parts of Iowa and
Minnesota, burdened with debt and almost despairing . . .
fastened the blame upon the bankers, the railways, the legislatures, the tariff, and monopolies . . ."[35] They united politically in the Granger and Populist movements. The new
parties were "anti-monopoly" and they were "reform"
movements.[36] The farmers organized coöperatives and negotiated overseas with the English Coöperative Union.[37]
They demanded that the Federal Government step in to
prevent the abuses of the railroads by helping to build a
Great Lakes-to-Gulf waterway or by constructing a railroad
from the Mississippi to the Atlantic seaboard.[38] They operated under slogans like "raise less corn and more *hell*."[39]
To get a hearing they resorted to sensational methods of
presentation.[40] "The Westerner has belonged to a minority
and has been compelled to accept the laws and institutions
made for other conditions or, at best, such modifications of
the laws as the Eastern senators and representatives could be
induced to agree to. About all the Westerner has been able

34. C. F. Adams Jr., "The Granger Movement," 120 *North American
Review* 394, 405 (1875).

35. Solon J. Buck, *The Granger Movement* (Cambridge, Mass., Harvard
University Press, 1933), p. 8.

36. *Ibid.*, p. 100.

37. *Ibid.*, pp. 239, 259.

38. Edward C. Kirkland, *A History of American Economic Life* (New
York, F. S. Crofts, 1932), p. 617.

39. *Ibid.*, p. 628.

40. Walter P. Webb, *Divided We Stand: The Crisis of a Frontierless
Democracy* (New York, Toronto, Farrar & Rinehart, 1937), p. 186.

to achieve has come through wheedling, cajolery, threats of radicalism, and the formation of third parties or of alliances with the minority party."[41]

"The ocean-bound East, lying at the mercy of bombarding fleets, fails to awaken the genuine sympathy of the inland West in appropriations for the navy. On the other hand, the West appeals to almost deaf ears when it pleads for generous sums for irrigating vast arid tracts, for surveying public lands and for developing the untouched resources of sparsely settled empires."[42]

That was all seventy or eighty years ago—in the United States. We must now reverse the roles of East and West as we turn to Scene No. 2.

In the 1940's and 1950's the newly independent nations of the East lived on an agricultural and raw-material producing economy. These Easterners had little capital and few industries. The ships which carried their products to the market were owned by Western business interests in New York, London, The Hague. Their national debts were owed to Western governments and their individual debts to local merchants and moneylenders who seemed equally remote from their interests. They were perplexed and looked eagerly about for something with which to find fault. They tended to fasten the blame on the wealthy countries of the West, identified as the "colonial powers." They united politically

41. Walter P. Webb, *The Great Plains* (Boston, Ginn and Co., 1931), p. 386.

42. Henry L. West, "Two Republics or One?" 162 *North American Review* 509, 510 (1896).

as in the Asian-Arab-African bloc. They negotiated overseas with underdeveloped countries of Latin America. Their
blocs were "anti-colonial" and they were "reform" movements. They demanded that the United Nations step in to
meet their needs by establishing SUNFED[43] with capital
contributed by the Western states. They operated under
slogans like "self-determination." To get a hearing they resorted to sensational charges and denunciations. They felt
that they belonged to a minority forced to accept the international law and international institutions developed by the
West, or at best such modifications as the Western members
of the United Nations could be induced to agree to. What
they were able to achieve came through oratory, appeals,
and threats of turning to Communism, and the formation
of blocs and voting with other minority blocs in the United
Nations. The Western powers, conscious of the danger
of the vast military might of the Soviet Union, failed to
awaken the genuine sympathy of the East when they promised to help with savings resulting from eventual agreement
on disarmament, but meanwhile turned deaf ears to pleas
for SUNFED or other schemes for using vast sums to irrigate
great arid tracts, for flood control, and for the industrializa-
tion of the underdeveloped lands.

DRAMA NO. 3. IN TWO SCENES

Little *v.* Big

The curtain rises on the first scene of our third little drama:
Lewis Dusenberry Gilbert, owner of ten shares in the Con-

43. Special United Nations Fund for Economic Development.

solidated Gas Company, attended the annual stockholders' meeting in 1933. Gilbert speaks: "The meeting was a disgrace. After the chairman had wasted an hour reading the annual report, which, of course, had already been mailed to the stockholders days before, I got up to ask a question, but before I had a chance to say anything, one of the officers sitting in the back of the room made a motion to adjourn. It was seconded and passed in no time . . . There I was, a part owner . . . and I had been treated like a tramp by these people, who were my employees . . ."[44]

An editorial in the Richmond, Virginia, *News-Leader* of January 24, 1953, speaks: "Time was . . . that the stockholder was regarded as a necessary nuisance. . . . Management ran things on a principle of 'tell the stockholders nothing.' "[45]

Time passes. Charles F. Robbins, President of A. G. Spalding Company, speaks in the company's annual report for 1948: "For the past four or five years, one stockholder has shown a particularly active interest in the affairs of the company, relating principally to the field of stockholder relations and stockholder interest. This stockholder, Mr. Lewis D. Gilbert, has made several suggestions, the majority of which the company has been very happy to adopt . . ."[46]

Scene No. 2 is set in Europe:

Serbia, Bulgaria, and Montenegro had only a little terri-

---

44. John Bainbridge, "Profiles, The Talking Stockholder, I," *The New Yorker,* December 11, 1948, p. 40.

45. Lewis D. and John J. Gilbert, *Fourteenth Annual Report of Stockholders Activities at Corporation Meetings, 1953* (New York, 1953), pp. 59–60.

46. Bainbridge, p. 44.

tory and an even smaller share of the military and political power of Europe in 1878 when the Congress of Berlin met to determine questions of general European interest and particularly questions vitally affecting those three small states. They were "not even permitted to appear before the Congress and express their views."[47] The Congress was managed by the Great Powers, who purported to represent Europe and to have the exclusive right to speak for it as they had in large measure since the Congress of Vienna in 1815.

In the 1950's Belgium, Denmark, Iceland, Luxembourg, the Netherlands, Norway, and Portugal had each only a little territory and an even smaller share of the political and military power of Europe, but they were all members of NATO and as such were consulted by the three Great Powers before they met with the Soviet Union in the Berlin Conference of 1954. In the previous year Burma, Guatemala, Honduras, Indonesia, and Mexico, over the opposition of most of the Great Powers, secured the passage of a resolution by the United Nations General Assembly asserting the Assembly's right to determine for itself whether a territory had ceased to be non-self-governing, no matter what the administering power said.[48]

Let us imagine Mr. Orthodox and Mr. Iconoclast discussing the three little dramas as they meet later in the latter's

47. Adolf Lande, "Revindication of the Principle of Legal Equality of States, 1871–1914," 62 *Political Science Quarterly* 258, 266–7 (1947).

48. See Sherman S. Hayden and Benjamin Rivlin, *Non-Self-Governing Territories, Status of Puerto Rico* (New York, Woodrow Wilson Foundation, 1954).

office. Ridiculous, says Orthodox, even to suggest that the
two scenes in any one of the dramas are comparable. International relations and law are big enough subjects now without dragging in domestic relations and disgruntled Western
farmers and professional minority stockholders. Would the
UN General Assembly or the International Court of Justice
consider the Nevada divorce law in passing on the French
pleas that, under the domestic jurisdiction clause of the
Charter, the United Nations cannot intervene in the Morocco question? And it wasn't Morocco that got the case on
the agenda anyway. There isn't even a transnational element
in Mary and Frank's divorce case, although I suppose Mary
could have gone to Mexico or Paris instead of to Reno. Are
we supposed to follow up the Drama of West *v.* East by
concluding that Krishna Menon is the international counterpart of William Jennings Bryan? And do you think that the
NATO Council is going to frame its procedures on the
basis of the SEC rules concerning a corporation's duty to
circulate minority proposals with its own proxy material?

Well, says Iconoclast, of course the dramatist has used
poetic license and I don't believe he intended that his analogies should be pressed to the bitter end. As for expanding
the field, he didn't go as far as McDougal and Lasswell. He
might well have brought in also the whole field of labor-
management relations where there are striking analogies to
international relations, as pointed out in Elmore Jackson's
Meeting of Minds. But as I see it, in the drama of M. *v.* F. he
is reminding us that there are many human situations where
those who are bound together, even for a long time, decide

that they want to separate. Sometimes the community decides that they must separate, as in the dissolution of a trust or the breakup of the German colonial empire after World War I and the freeing of the Italian colonies in North Africa after World War II. Maybe the dramatist thinks there's a lesson to be learned from the preface to Duclos' *Histoire de Louis XI* where Duclos says: "We see on the theater of the world a certain number of scenes which succeed each other in endless repetition: where we see the same faults followed regularly by the same misfortunes, we may reasonably think that if we could have known the first we might have avoided the others."[49] Duclos wasn't worried by the fact that the cast of characters is constantly changing.

But I grant you, says Iconoclast, the divorce case analogy is a little farfetched. The antagonisms between regions within a state seem to me much more comparable to their international counterparts. A little change in history can make an internal problem an international one. The Grangers and Populists did not try to secede, but the South, with much the same economic distrust of the North, did; and if the Confederacy had won, the economic problem would not have been solved but would have become international. Just before the Civil War Jefferson Davis found a parallel between our western frontier and the French occupation of Algeria.[50]

Farmers in Virginia today may not think they are very

49. Quoted by Carl L. Becker as Storrs lecturer in 1931, *The Heavenly City of the Eighteenth-Century Philosophers* (New Haven, Yale University Press, 1932), p. 95.

50. Webb, *The Great Plains,* p. 195.

much like the peasants who work the rice fields in Southeast Asia, but listen to this: ". . . the impecunious farmer purchased all his supplies during a year on credit from a merchant who relied on the sale of the forthcoming crop for payment. . . . As a result when the farmer came to balance up at the end of the year he frequently found himself still in debt to the merchant, after the disposal of his crop. In many cases the annual residue of debt increased year by year until finally crops, stock, farm, and all were absorbed by the ruinous system."

And this: "Compelled by poverty to convert into ready cash his usually small share [of the crop] he sells it at prices below production costs. . . . He goes deeper into debt with no hope for salvation."

And this: ". . . the cultivator frequently finds his credit exhausted just when the land is about to repay the initial expenditures made for developing it . . . The inexperienced . . . farmer almost inevitably was forced to default on his debt and to lose his property."

The first description is by Solon Buck of the southern agricultural class, both white and black, after the Civil War.[51] The second is of the Philippine rice farmer and the third of the operation of the Chettyars, the Indian moneylenders of Burma, both taken from Erich H. Jacoby's *Agrarian Unrest in South East Asia*.[52]

If you consider the Southeast Asian situations each by itself, you find the added complication of what one might call

51. *The Granger Movement*, p. 6.
52. (New York, Columbia University Press, 1949), pp. 210 and 80.

a local transnational situation, since the merchants and moneylenders are foreigners—Chinese or Indians. The basic economic hostility might therefore turn into racial or national animosity.

The cleavage between the backward agricultural South in Italy and the cosmopolitan industrial North, Iconoclast argues, was apparent as an international difference before unification and as an internal problem thereafter. The problems and the feelings of the impoverished peasants of the Mezzogiorno are quite comparable to those of the "teeming masses" of Asia. The differences between the upper and lower Sudan became a problem in the three-cornered international relations of the United Kingdom, Egypt, and the emerging Sudanese state. In Nigeria and the Gold Coast the economic clash between the uplanders and the coastal people existed in tribal days, continued under British rule, and will not end with the dawn of independence. The line between the internal and the transnational is rather thin. One's idea of what constitutes a "region" is apt to be artificial and highly subjective. The people in Boston and New York today might quite properly feel that they have a closer identity of interest with the people of India than their grandfathers felt about the farmers of Iowa. The connection between domestic tranquillity and aid to underdeveloped areas has come to be appreciated in the United States and in Italy, and the international application of the same principle which we now call Point Four or technical assistance was one of the planks in Colonel House's program in 1914 for alleviating Anglo-German rivalry and preventing the outbreak of

World War I.[53] The Truman Point Four plan was an international application of the Triple A program of the New Deal in relation to the cotton planters of the South. The pendulum swings back again to the regional internal application, as the *New York Times* on October 25, 1955, reported from Denver that "President Eisenhower will ask Congress next year for a domestic version of the Point Four technical assistance program to aid the nation's chronically depressed areas."

As for the minority stockholders, continues Iconoclast, one reads quite a bit these days about "corporate democracy,"[54] meaning increasing attention to the demands of those stockholders as against the management into whose hands control had passed, as demonstrated by Berle and Means.[55] At the same time you hear about the democratization of the United Nations, as the broadly based General Assembly takes on more and more authority through such measures as the Uniting for Peace Resolution and the supervision of non-self-governing territories. Maybe that's a general human trend.

You can trace, says Iconoclast, the invasion of the domestic realm of the national state by the growing concern for minorities, human rights, and the genocide convention, and the administration of colonial or non-self-governing

53. Edward H. Buehrig, *Woodrow Wilson and the Balance of Power* (Bloomington, Indiana University Press, 1955), p. 187.

54. "When Is a Stockholder a Nuisance?" *Fortune, 49* (March 1954), 86.

55. Adolf A. Berle and Gardiner C. Means, *The Modern Corporation and Private Property* (New York, Chicago, Washington, Commerce Clearing House, 1932).

peoples. Compare this with the invasion of corporate privacy through the courts' protection of the rights of minority stockholders since, as Lilienthal points out, "Even a routine price increase, that must have seemed to the steel companies a matter of their 'private business,' not long ago created such a furor among purchasers generally that it was necessary for steel's management to justify its prices before a joint Congressional committee."[56]

It is a recent and still restricted development in the field of United States corporation law that administrative agencies of government should have the quasi-judicial power to pass upon the validity of claims for mismanagement of corporations, as is now in certain situations within the power of the Interstate Commerce Commission and the Securities and Exchange Commission.[57] Stockholders' suits have been denounced as "strike suits"[58] and have, on the other hand, been heralded as having "accomplished much in policing the corporate system" and having "educated corporate directors."[59] But the law is still powerless to intervene in many corporate "internal affairs," as Timberg complains.[60]

56. David E. Lilienthal, *Big Business: A New Era* (New York, Harper & Brothers, 1952), p. 29.

57. George D. Hornstein, "A New Forum for Stockholders," 45 *Columbia Law Review* 35, 36 (1945).

58. Franklin A. Wood, *Survey and Report Regarding Stockholders' Derivative Suits* (Special Committee on Corporate Litigation, Chamber of Commerce of the State of New York, 1944).

59. Judge Rifkind in Brendle *v.* Smith, 46 F. Supp. 522, 525 (S.D.N.Y. 1942).

60. "International Combines and National Sovereigns," p. 580.

Forty years ago it was unthinkable that a state administering colonies should be called to international account for its management. The case of the humanitarian intervention provoked by the atrocities in the Belgian Congo in 1906 might be considered an exception, but at least on the part of the United States concern was manifested quietly and largely behind the scenes; other states could justify their interest on the basis of general treaties.[61] Today in the United Nations the Trusteeship Council has a quasi-judicial power to pass upon claims by inhabitants of trust territories, or by other states, that the territories are being mismanaged. Any member of the United Nations may, in the Fourth Committee of the General Assembly, challenge the management not only of trust territories but also of non-self-governing territories, as vigorously as the Gilbert brothers or Mrs. Wilma Soss, president of the Federation of Women Shareholders in American Business, heckle the management of Bethlehem Steel, Standard of New Jersey, or the Pennsylvania Railroad. The administrator of a colonial area is often outraged when representatives of other members of the United Nations, who, in his opinion, have no experience or knowledge or responsibility behind their views, suggest changes in the administration of a trust territory. *Mutatis mutandis,* the administrator might reply, as Charles M. Schwab, chairman of the board of Bethlehem Steel, replied when Lewis Dusenberry Gilbert suggested that he retire on a pension. "It is a sad moment," said Schwab, "when anyone

61. Philip C. Jessup, *Elihu Root* (New York, Dodd, Mead, 1938), 2, 61ff.

makes such a suggestion. In the thirty-five years since I founded Bethlehem, I have devoted my entire life and energy to building it up. It is my lifework and I am proud of it."[62] The critics of the colonial administrators profess, no doubt genuinely, a devotion to the native peoples. The general counsel of the New York Central Railroad once asked the assiduous minority stockholder Mrs. Wilma Soss (she owned ten shares of Central stock) why she caused so much trouble. "Because I love the Central," said Mrs. Soss, to which the railroad official replied, "Will you please go away and love some other railroad?"[63] Some of the colonial administrators have suggested that the critics should spend their love on some of their own indigenous backward peoples like the Indians of the Andes and the Amazon or the Nagas in Assam,[64] a further example, by the way, of an intranational counterpart to a transnational situation.

To be sure, the United Nations is not a corporation and the states members are not shareholders and the analogy is very far from perfect. But the modern state, like the big corporation, has developed, for different reasons, a new sensitivity to public pressures; and the law (United Nations Charter or United States statute) has taken account of the new social consciousness. During the great anthracite coal strike of 1902 a business magnate could say: "The rights and

62. John Bainbridge, "Profiles, The Talking Stockholder, II," *The New Yorker,* December 18, 1948, p. 33.

63. "For Love," *The New Yorker,* April 24, 1954, p. 26.

64. See F. Van Langenhove, *La question des aborigènes aux Nations Unies: La thèse belge* (Brussels, Institut Royal Colonial Belge, Section des Sciences Morales et Politiques, Mémoires, 1954), vol. 37, fasc. 4.

interests of the laboring man will be protected and cared for—not by the labor agitators, but by the Christian men to whom God in His infinite wisdom has given the control of the property interests of this country."[65] There was a public outcry, not so much against the philosophy as against what many considered blasphemy. It had not been many years since Commodore Vanderbilt had said, "The public be damned." At the same period colonial administrators and missionaries were cheerfully and sometimes sanctimoniously shouldering the "white man's burden," and with frugal paternalism seeing to it that every Gunga Din should have at least "a piece of twisty rag" and that every Polynesian human curve should be concealed beneath a mou-mou.

Again one must agree that the minority shareholder has a definite proprietary stake in the affairs of "his" corporation, even though he own but ten out of two million shares of stock, while it is not always obvious that the complainants against colonial administrations are fired by sheer humanitarianism, which in some instances they could more successfully practice at home. The fact remains that, from Woodrow Wilson and the League mandate system on through Franklin Roosevelt and the United Nations trusteeship and allied systems, the manifestations of the awakening social conscience have appeared simultaneously in the domestic and in the international fields. The New Freedom and the New Deal were not sold only in the domestic market.

Poverty is a perennial weed in the garden of human societies. But, as Webster points out, "Poverty is a relative term;

65. See Jessup, *Elihu Root, 1,* p. 273.

what is poverty to a monarch would be competence for a
laborer." A Germany could feel poor for want of colonies
or *Lebensraum*. A Chile or an Indonesia feels poor for want
of capital to develop its internal economy. The problems
arising from these current yearnings or demands of the underdeveloped countries must be described as transnational
rather than merely international, since they involve the relations of, say, Indonesia not only to the United States for
example but also to the private sources of American capital
and to such intergovernmental organizations as the International Bank for Reconstruction and Development. They
are characterized by some bitterness and by attitudes on the
part of the have-nots which the haves consider quite unreasonable. "In certain circles abroad the dispensing of aid
by the United States is regarded as not only a duty, but a
privilege."[66] No responsible official of the United States has
ever been in the position of the straw man who is knocked
down on the assumption that he advocated foreign aid pro-
grams in order to buy friends or favor for the United States.

When such issues as we have been describing attain certain
proportions or degrees of intensity, something is done about
it. If it is not done by the haves, the have-nots may resort to
domestic violence, or to international war, or to the General
Assembly of the United Nations. When the action is taken
by the haves it is normally legal action. It may be a treaty
between Great Britain and Germany concerning areas of
colonial expansion in Africa, an Interstate Commerce Act,

66. Edward S. Mason, *Promoting Economic Development: The United
States and Southern Asia* (Claremont, Cal., Claremont College, 1955), p. 15.

the Triple A, the Articles of Agreement of the International Bank, or a resolution of the General Assembly in favor of SUNFED. The problem is not settled by law in the sense that poverty is outlawed, but, by taxation or otherwise, those who have may be required to give to those who have not. When foreign capital moved in to underdeveloped countries in response to economic opportunity rather than political decision, international law developed rules relative to the protection of that property to the point where Max Huber (as Arbitrator between Great Britain and Spain) could say: "The diplomatic protection of nationals against injuries suffered in a foreign country is one of the most important institutions of international law."[67] To redress the balance the Calvo and Drago Doctrines were evolved. Today balances are sought through a United Nations commission on restrictive business practices. As already noted, the Point Four program of the United States looked outward beyond the frontiers of the United States, but some two decades earlier the Triple A program performed a similar service for the depressed cotton areas of the Southland within the United States. Mason points out[68] that in the domestic sphere various forms of income distribution have taken place not as the "result of voluntary offerings by the well-to-do; it has been compelled by government. And in the international arena there is to date no power that is likely to be able to compel well-to-do nations to share their substance with the less well-to-do." No power indeed, in the sense of

67. 2 *UN Reports of International Arbitral Awards* 615, 636.
68. *Promoting Economic Development.*

a governmental instrumentality whose fiat is law, but perhaps just as much power in the form of the pressures generated by Communist-non-Communist rivalries, the consciousness of need for security, and perhaps economic or humanitarian pressures. The successful operation of the United Nations Technical Assistance program exercised a sufficiently powerful leverage to induce the laggard participation of the Soviet Union. The purchase of arms by Egypt from the Soviet bloc, or Soviet offers of financial aid to construct a dam on the Nile, may be just as powerful in compelling the United States and Great Britain to supply the demand as if there were an international legislature which made such supply legally obligatory.

2. THE POWER TO DEAL WITH THE PROBLEMS

IN *The Lotus* CASE the Permanent Court of International Justice said: ". . . all that can be required of a State is that it should not overstep the limits which international law places upon its jurisdiction; within these limits, its title to exercise jurisdiction rests in its sovereignty."[1]

There has been a great deal of ink spilled on paper to prove or disprove that there is a legal obligation to obey international law. In orthodox theory the individual is not so obligated, because international law ignores him and addresses itself only to states. In the same theory the state is so obligated, although the reasons advanced in support of that proposition are many and varied. National courts have drawn on international law and, again with various theoretical justifications, have found in international law the rule for decision of cases. No one doubts that the appropriate authorities of a state may by constitutional or legislative enactment direct that this shall be done. Witness the wholesale incorporation of international law by the constitutions of the German Federal Republic, Austria, and other states,[2] and the common statutory enactments of the rules providing

---

1. P.C.I.J., ser. A, no. 10 (1927), p. 19.
2. Samples are given in Herbert W. Briggs, *The Law of Nations* (2d ed., New York, Appleton-Century-Crofts, 1952), p. 58.

for diplomatic immunities. The whys, the wherefores, and the hows of this process are still interesting fields of exploration, but we are off on a different expedition.[3] Our present purpose is to examine which authorities deal effectively with which transnational situations. In familiar language this question may be approached as a matter of jurisdiction.

In most discussions of jurisdiction a distinction is drawn between criminal and civil cases, and the jurisdictional rules differ according to the category in which the case is put. International law books generally deal only with penal (criminal) jurisdiction except for such questions as those of maritime and air jurisdiction and the exemptions from civil jurisdiction which flow from the doctrines of sovereign and diplomatic immunity. Books on conflict of laws, like the American Law Institute's *Restatement,* generally confine their attention to civil jurisdiction.[4] One finds it said that public international law does not regulate conflict of laws, and a terminological device is utilized by some writers to differentiate international questions of criminal law by calling it "international penal law"; this is indeed the title of one chapter of the Bustamente Code.

In general the distinction between civil and criminal wrongs seems clear, but this is not always true; and even recently it has been necessary for the Supreme Court to de-

3. To avoid misunderstanding I would interpolate that after a few years of practical contact with international affairs, and after further reflection, I find no reason to change my view in *A Modern Law of Nations* (ch. 1) that international law is a valuable and valid legal system which, on the whole, is as well observed as national law.

4. The *Restatement* devotes four pages out of 738 to crimes.

cide which tag to put on proceedings. The cases involved contempt proceedings which may be either civil or criminal; the procedural rules applicable differ according to which type of contempt is involved. While the cases are therefore limited to the points of procedure, some of the language used in the opinions illustrates the point that the line between civil and criminal may at the least require careful analysis. In 1922 the Court, speaking through Mr. Justice Brandeis, declared: "Where a fine is imposed partly as compensation to the complainant and partly as punishment, the criminal feature of the order is dominant and fixes its character for purposes of review."[5] In 1941 the Court, by Mr. Justice Douglas, quoted from a decision two years earlier to the effect that "While particular acts do not always readily lend themselves to classification as civil or criminal contempts, a contempt is considered civil when the punishment is wholly remedial, serves only the purposes of the complainant, and is not intended as a deterrent to offenses against the public."[6] Six years later in the John L. Lewis case Chief Justice Vinson said: "Common sense would recognize that conduct can amount to both civil and criminal contempt. The same acts may justify a court in resorting to coercive and to punitive measures."[7] The Union Tool and United Mine Workers cases seem to suggest that the element of punish-

5. Union Tool Co. *v.* Wilson, 259 U.S. 107, 110 (1922).

6. Nye *v.* United States, 313 U.S. 33, 42 (1941) citing McCrone *v.* United States, 307 U.S. 61, 64 (1939).

7. United States *v.* United Mine Workers of America, 330 U.S. 258, 298-9 (1947).

ment brands the action as criminal, but in civil cases punitive or exemplary damages are familiar. Brandeis noted that a fine may be compensatory, and in the McCrone case the Court indicated that punishment may serve "only the purposes of the complainant" and not "as a deterrent to offenses against the public," while, on the other hand, in some civil cases extra damages may serve the purposes of the state precisely as a deterrent. Walton Hamilton has pointed out that "The state quite consciously may make a private action in tort the instrument of a public purpose. It may by legislative act make the wrongdoer liable for actions or practices which it seeks to prevent to the extent of double or even quadruple the amount of the actual damage." He cites statutes having this design in such cases as negligent setting of a fire, malicious prosecution, forcible entry and detainer, and also actions for triple damages under the Sherman Act. "The provision for a multiple of damages may be a substitute for or a supplement to criminal prosecution."[8] In nonsupport cases against deserting husbands the punitive and deterrent elements are mixed with the compensatory. But jurisdictional requirements do not always vary with the identification of such legislative punitive purposes; the actions are still tagged as civil or criminal and the respective rules of jurisdiction apply. In the Supreme Court contempt cases the distinction had to be drawn in order to determine whether the proper procedural steps had been followed, which in turn depended on whether the proceeding was civil or

8. Walton H. Hamilton, article on "Damages" in *Encyclopaedia of the Social Sciences* (1935), *4*, 699.

criminal. In the Nye case a jurisdictional problem was posed, and in the United Mine Workers case part of the Supreme Court's holding was that the defendants were properly tried by the lower court without a jury. In the familiar Blackmer case the defendant was judged *in absentia*. Granted that certain rules of constitutional law in the United States require certain procedures which conform to the standards of due process, the question may be asked whether there is fundamentally good reason for insisting on different jurisdictional requirements in civil and criminal cases and indeed for relegating the two types of jurisdiction to two different bodies of law—international law and conflict of laws.

"Jurisdiction is power," said Mr. Justice Holmes.[9] But it is as complicated to define power as it is to define jurisdiction.[10] The territorial concept was strongly rooted in Holmes's mind. He spoke of the "old notion of personal sovereignty" which was kept alive "to some extent." There were "startling applications" of the notion that "English statutes bind British subjects everywhere." "All legislation is *prima facie* territorial," and statutes should be construed as "intended to be confined . . . to the territorial limits over which the lawmaker has general and legitimate power." Law, he thought, is generally "addressed to persons living within the power of the courts." These quotations from the familiar Banana Company case[11] are representative of the territorial

9. Michigan Trust Co. *v.* Ferry, 228 U.S. 346, 356 (1913).

10. I have dealt with part of this problem in "Power, Facts and Law," *Proceedings of the American Society of International Law* (1955), p. 1.

11. American Banana Co. *v.* United Fruit Co., 213 U.S. 347 (1909).

point of view which was long dominant in Anglo-American legal thought.

One need not quarrel with the Supreme Court's interpretation of the Sherman Antitrust Act, but the facts of that case present an interesting transnational situation. Two American corporations, competing for the banana business in Central America, were involved in the only too familiar game of influencing the political action of the local foreign governments, in this case Colombia, Panama, and Costa Rica. There were many international complications in the background, since the events described in the plaintiff's complaint took place just before and after Theodore Roosevelt "took Panama" in order to have the Panama Canal built. Only seven or eight years before, Secretary Olney had told Great Britain that the fiat of the United States was law on this continent "upon the subjects to which it confines its interposition." But the plaintiff Banana Company said that it had been unsuccessful in its efforts to secure the interposition of the United States on its behalf, and the case before the Supreme Court was not an international one in the true sense of that word. Since the acts complained of occurred in Central America, Holmes said they occurred "outside the jurisdiction of the United States." But if jurisdiction is power, it is perfectly clear that in those days the United States had as much power in Costa Rica as it had in West Virginia which is only a third larger. Holmes, however, was not talking about that kind of power, because he said that Costa Rica acted "by virtue of its sovereign power" and "The very meaning of sovereignty is that the decree of the sovereign makes law."[12] But he might have gone on to repeat his view that the sovereign makes law only within its own territory where, to use Chief Justice Marshall's phrase, its jurisdiction is "necessarily exclusive and absolute."[13] As one looks at the problem today one comes to the conclusion that this is by no means necessarily so and that in fact the sovereign's power is neither exclusive nor absolute within its own territory, and that this is true whether one is talking in terms of legal or extralegal power. Nor is its power (jurisdiction) confined to its territory. The "old notion of personal sovereignty" could, of course, have been relied on by Congress to direct United States citizens, including corporations, to act or not to act in a certain manner wherever they might be. This "old notion" is indeed both older and newer than the territorial theory. "The history of all laws opens with an entirely personal conception of law: every man possessed only the rights and duties with which the laws of his own tribe, city, or class invested him, and could not be judged by any other."[14] So in the Germanic legal system of Western Europe law was tribal, i.e. personal. In the nomadic period it could hardly have been otherwise, but when the principle of territoriality developed in the Middle Ages it was adopted with surprising rapidity.[15] But

12. Olney had also said the United States was "practically sovereign upon this continent."

13. The *Schooner Exchange v.* McFaddon, 7 Cranch 116, 135 (1812).

14. W. E. Becket, "The Exercise of Criminal Jurisdiction Over Foreigners," 6 *British Yearbook of International Law* 44, 51 (1925).

15. Josef Kohler, *Internationales Strafrecht* (Stuttgart, Ferdinand Enke, 1917), p. 20.

even in the early feudal period there was "no territorial law as we today understand it—a body of law applying to all within the land, whether foreigners or not"; the system of personal law continued.[16] Because thieves, swindlers, and murderers traveled from city to city and each city was equally affected by their depredations, the malefactors were likely to be punished in whatever city they were found regardless of the place where they had committed the crime. Given the connotation which the name Nuremberg has for us today, it is interesting to find it recorded that in the 15th century when such malefactors were found in that city "They used to send word to the authorities of the individuals' earlier residence and inquire about their wrongdoings."[17] Strict territoriality of law was also not consistent with the fact that feudal ties cut across national frontiers and thus had a transnational aspect.[18]

In another geographical area where Moslem law ruled, the emphasis was also personal rather than territorial, and in Islam it was deemed proper that many different bodies of law should be applicable within the same territory to peoples of different religions—Moslem, Christian, Jew.[19] This sys-

16. Abraham C. Bernheim, *The History of the Law of Aliens* (New York, J. F. Pearson, Printer, 1885), pp. 19, 32; E. Munroe Smith, article on "Law of Nationality" in *Cyclopaedia of Political Science, Political Economy, and of the Political History of the United States,* ed. John J. Lalor (Chicago, 1883), 2, 943.

17. Kohler, p. 45.

18. Nussbaum uses the adjective "transnational" in describing this situation in *A Concise History of the Law of Nations,* p. 22.

19. Majid Khadduri, *War and Peace in the Law of Islam* (Baltimore, The Johns Hopkins Press, 1955), pp. 141ff; Najib Armanazi, *L'Islam et le droit international* (Paris, Librairie Picart, 1929), p. 48.

tem facilitated the conclusion of the later treaties known as the "capitulations" under which Western Europeans and Americans lived in Moslem countries under their own laws. In contrast to the "unequal" treaties granting extraterritoriality in China and Japan, these treaties were not surrenders to Western power and were called capitulations because they were divided into numbered *capitula* or brief chapters.[20] And so in 1952 we find the International Court of Justice speaking of "the history of the old conflict between two concepts of law and jurisdiction: the one based upon persons and the other upon territory. The right of consular jurisdiction was designed to provide for a situation in which Moroccan law was essentially personal in character and could not be applied to foreigners."[21] Until recently the same personal system was to be found in British and Dutch colonies.

Today the common-law countries consider the territorial principle basic, but they have adopted and are constantly extending their applications of the personal principle, which has thus become for them the newer principle. Civil-law countries emphasize the personal principle but also accept the territorial. The territorial emphasis in English common law has been traced to the insular position of England, having no international land boundaries and knowing only the boundaries between counties. For convenience of assembling evidence, and ensuring the attendance of witnesses and

20. Nussbaum, p. 55.

21. Case concerning rights of nationals of the United States of America in Morocco, Judgment of August 27th, 1952: I.C.J. Reports 1952, p. 176 at p. 191.

allowing the neighbors of the vicinage to try the facts as jurors, the place where the deed was done was obviously the most suitable; and so a rule of venue grew into a principle of territorial jurisdiction.[22] This oversimplified statement may be criticized but is reasonably descriptive. One finds recurrent emphasis upon the importance of questions of proof at the place of the crime. As Lauterpacht puts it: "Territoriality of jurisdiction is a rule of convenience in the sphere of evidence. It is not a requirement of justice or even a necessary postulate of the sovereignty of the State."[23]

The convenient rule of evidence has not, however, hindered the expansion of the territorial theory into its subjective and objective applications, which are easily accepted by strict territorialists although very distantly related to the problem of proof. The original justification would hardly apply, for example, to John Doe whose friend Richard Roe calls on him in Buffalo and asks him to act as his second in a duel to which he has been challenged in Canada by William Soanso of Montreal; John goes with Richard to Canada, and holds his jacket while he is mortally wounded in the duel by William. On his return to Buffalo John could be indicted for murder in the second degree under Section 1047 of Chapter 41 of the Consolidated Laws of New York

22. Thomas P. Fry, *The International and National Competence of Australian Parliaments to Legislate in Respect of Extra-Territorial Crime (Including War Crimes)*, University of Queensland Papers, Faculty of Law, vol. *1*, no. 2 (1947), p. 9.

23. H. Lauterpacht, "Allegiance, Diplomatic Protection and Criminal Jurisdiction over Aliens," 9 *Cambridge Law Journal* 330, 348, n. 61 (1945–47).

(1923).[24] And the same William could later be punished in New York under the territorial theory, if while passing through New York he formed the intent to beat his dog to death and carried out his intent in Canada.[25]

When a state wishes to find and punish the "whodunit" it follows strange fictional clues to territoriality. Thus a German court convicted a man of sedition for crying *Vive la France* in France near the German border, on the ground that the cry took effect in Germany because it was heard there.[26] A Georgia court sustained the sanctity of the territorial principle in upholding the jurisdiction of the Georgia courts to prosecute for assault with intent to murder, a man who stood on the South Carolina bank of the Savannah River and shot at a man in a boat on the Georgia side, the

24. "Sec. 1047. A person who, by previous appointment made within the state, fights a duel without the state, and in so doing inflicts a wound upon his antagonist, whereof the person injured dies; or who engages or participates in such a duel, as second or assistant to either party, is guilty of murder in the second degree, and may be indicted, tried, and convicted in any county of the state."

25. New York, *Cons. Laws,* 1923, c. 41. "Sec. 195. A person who leaves this state with intent to elude any of the provisions of this article or to commit any act out of this state which is prohibited by them, or who, being a resident of this state, does any act out of this state, pursuant to such intent, which would be punishable under such circumstances if committed within this state, is punishable in the same manner as if such act had been committed within this state." Both examples are taken from "Research in International Law under the Auspices of the Faculty of the Harvard Law School, II: Jurisdiction with Respect to Crime" (hereinafter cited as Harvard Research), published in 29 *American Journal of International Law,* suppl. p. 485 (1935).

26. *Ibid.,* p. 494.

bullet having missed the intended victim and struck Georgian water. The court said: "Of course, the presence of the accused within this State is essential to make his act one which is done in this State; but the presence need not be actual. It may be constructive. . . . So, if a man in the State of South Carolina criminally fires a ball into the State of Georgia, law regards him as accompanying the ball, and as being represented by it up to the point where it strikes . . . He started across the river with his leaden messenger, and was operating it up to the moment when it ceased to move, and was therefore, in a legal sense, after the ball crossed the State line up to the moment that it stopped, in Georgia."[27]

As soon as one passes from the reality to the fictional basis of "constructive presence" one has opened the door to wide extensions of jurisdiction. If a man theoretically accompanies a bullet, or a package of poison candy, or a swindling letter, he may also accompany a plot hatched abroad against the security of the state although the plot was wholly abortive. At this point the tendency is to jump over the territorial traces and admit another basis of jurisdiction, that is, the protective principle. The transition is the easier once it is agreed—as it is—that the personal theory is also acceptable.

The personal theory of jurisdiction has no connection, real or fictional, with the territorial theory. "By virtue of the ·obligations of citizenship," said Chief Justice Hughes for the Supreme Court in the Blackmer case,[28] "the United States retained its authority over him, and he was bound by

27. Simpson *v*. State, 92 Ga. 41, 43, 46 (1893).
28. Blackmer *v*. United States, 284 U.S. 421, 436 (1932).

its laws made applicable to him in a foreign country." The Banana case, the Chief Justice explained, was a matter of "construction, not of legislative power." Although the legislation of many countries circumscribes by conditions and safeguards the exercise of jurisdiction to punish nationals for crimes committed abroad, since each state is free to determine for itself whether it will adopt any such limits, the Harvard Research is correct only to a certain extent in saying that existing limitations tend "to confirm the opinion that jurisdiction based upon nationality is properly regarded as subsidiary to the territorial jurisdiction of the State where the crime was committed."[29] The Harvard Draft accepts the rule found in the laws of some countries that, even if the person was an alien when the crime was committed, he may be punished by a state of which he has the nationality at the time of prosecution, and conversely the state may punish an alien who was a citizen at the time the crime was committed. In other words, the power of the state may reach into a man's past and into his future. Some states assert jurisdiction if the individual's connection with the state is merely that of domicile regardless of nationality and the domiciliary tie is indeed historically the older claim. In the case of Lord Haw-Haw the English court proceeded on the theory that an alien could continue to owe allegiance even while abroad and therefore could be punished for treason committed abroad.[30]

29. Harvard Research, p. 531.
30. Joyce *v.* Director of Public Prosecutions [1946] A.C. 347, discussed by Lauterpacht, p. 330.

Ordinarily one thinks of the tie of citizenship as involving a rather close relationship between the person and the state, but this is not necessarily the case. The United States Government, in its long battle to establish the right of expatriation, found it necessary to agree that citizenship might well be a sham. Many immigrants came to the United States for the purpose of escaping obligations, such as those for military service, in their native lands. Having stayed here the minimum length of time required by our naturalization laws, they would return to the ancestral farm or village and expect to thumb their noses at the recruiting officer. By treaty and by amendment of our own statutes we agreed that this was fraudulent, and the individual in question was "presumed" to have expatriated himself or might have his naturalization canceled. The tie between the United States and a presumed expatriate would not be a reasonable basis for the exercise of personal jurisdiction on the nationality principle. Neither is it reasonable for a totalitarian state which denies the right of expatriation to assert jurisdiction on the personality principle over one who has succeeded in escaping many years before and who has become permanently domiciled, even if not naturalized, in the United States. The International Court of Justice refused to recognize the right of Liechtenstein to espouse the Nottebohm claim against Guatemala, when it appeared that Nottebohm's naturalization in Liechtenstein was not based upon any "bond of attachment" between him and that country.[31] A

31. Nottebohm Case (second phase), Judgment of April 6th, 1955: I.C.J. Reports 1955, p. 4 at p. 26.

United States District Court considered that Fritz von Opel's naturalization in Liechtenstein was a "citizenship of convenience," since he had never been in the country except when traveling through it and never took an oath of allegiance to it, although he did pay some $10,000 for his naturalization there.[32] An international court or a national court might equally well question the fictional applications of the territorial theory. But instead of being nominal, nationality may, unlike domicile, be dual, and the man with dual nationality might be subject to conflicting legal precepts of equal validity.

There are still other ties than citizenship, domicile, or allegiance which are invoked in support of personal jurisdiction. The case of an alien who is serving a state abroad as a public functionary seems to be a case of obvious reasonableness and is covered by the legislation of many states. The Harvard Research approves this basis and also the special case of jurisdiction over an alien engaged as one of the personnel of a national ship or aircraft, even though the offense is not committed aboard the ship or aircraft. This claim to jurisdiction (rarely asserted) is again based on the tie, sometimes described as temporary allegiance, which the crew member owes to the flag state.[33]

As one passes to the theory of protective jurisdiction, one finds a varied practice but general acceptance of a basic principle which indeed antedates the establishment of the

32. Uebersee Finanz-Korporation *v.* Brownell, 133 F. Supp. 615, 619 (D. D.C. 1955).
33. Harvard Research, p. 542.

modern state and the emergence of the territorial theory.[34] Here one embarks on the broad sea of acts affecting the security and integrity of the state, and more and more ships of state are to be encountered on that sea. Lauterpacht suggests that the increase in the exercise of this type of jurisdiction is due to "technical developments in the field of communications" as a result of which "the importance of mere physical distance—and therefore of the territorial principle—has correspondingly diminished."[35] While the principle is soundly based and now generally accepted, it is subject, more than any other acknowledged principle of jurisdiction, to extravagant extensions of state power. For example, during World War I France condemned to twenty years imprisonment a Spanish citizen, captain of a Spanish merchantman, for correspondence in Spain with the subjects of an enemy power.[36] Under Hitler's regime in Germany it was held that the law for the purity of the German blood justified the prosecution in Germany of a Jewish alien who had extramarital intercourse with a German girl in Czechoslovakia.[37] The United States recognizes that Communism is dangerous to its peace and safety but does not prosecute an alien for being a Communist behind the Iron Curtain. If it should undertake to do so, one might expect the Soviet authorities to prosecute any American they could

34. See above and Harvard Research, p. 543.

35. Lauterpacht, p. 344.

36. Harvard Research, p. 558.

37. 11 *Zeitschrift für ausländisches öffentliches Recht und Völkerrecht* 576 (1942–43).

lay hands on for practicing capitalism in the United States. But we have not yet reached the point of extending the Nuremberg principle of guilt by participation in a conspiracy to wage aggressive war to enacting a United States statute punishing a nonresident alien for guilt by participation in the Communist conspiracy to wage cold war, although he may be less directly penalized through our immigration laws. Yet the provisions of many existing penal codes based on the protective principle could be stretched that far. It would cause resentment, but not surprise, if the Chinese authorities in Peiping condemned an American citizen on such grounds. This is not to say that such a proceeding should be considered "right" or "just" or "proper," but it points the difficulty of drawing a hard and fast line once one accepts the protective principle. Whether such extreme examples of the exercise of jurisdiction should be acquiesced in or resisted depends on judgments based on considerations other than traditional notions of sovereignty and jurisdiction.

It is apparent that the foregoing cases of exercise of state jurisdiction which arouse discussion, and perhaps criticism, are those which involve some transnational aspect. There still lingers the notion that within its own territory the jurisdiction of a nation is necessarily exclusive and absolute. To make an even stronger case, assume that within its own territory the state is exercising its power over its own citizens with respect to acts planned, performed, and taking effect within its own territory. At this point one must be reminded of the new international interest, or meddling if you will,

in matters which once were thought to be essentially domestic. Although the United States Government does not
agree, the international movement in favor of human rights
and against such specific crimes as genocide (which may be
wholly territorial) has considerable support. Leaving aside
the question of the legal standing of the United Nations Universal Declaration of Human Rights, and admitting that the
Covenants on Human Rights are still adrafting in United
Nations committees, one interested in the general problem
may consider what has been done in this field in Europe.

Since July 5, 1955, the European Commission of Human
Rights has been competent to examine individual appeals,
that is, applications lodged by any person, nongovernmental
organization, or group of individuals claiming to be the
victim of a violation of the Convention for the Protection
of Human Rights and Fundamental Freedoms signed at
Rome on November 4, 1950. The competence exists only
when the state charged with a violation has expressly accepted the competence of the commission to hear such peti-
tions; by the end of 1955 there had been such acceptances
by Sweden, Ireland, Denmark, Iceland, the German
Federal Republic, Belgium, and Norway. The Commission
met for the first time at Strasbourg, with the President of the
High Court of Justice of Luxembourg in the chair, and examined preliminarily sixty-three of the eighty applications
which had been lodged. The results of the investigation are
interesting and not very alarming to those who are devoted
to the cause of exclusive national domestic authority:

"44 applications were rejected, being considered outside

the competence of the Commission, for example because they related to facts not covered by the Convention or because the facts alleged by the applicants occurred before the Convention entered into force;

"18 applications were reserved for further study as to their admissibility;

"1 application has been transmitted to the State against which complaint has been lodged, so that this Government may formulate its observations as to the admissibility of the application."[38]

The European Court of Human Rights has not yet been set up since the required number of acceptances of its compulsory jurisdiction have not been deposited. Final binding judgments cannot therefore yet be made.

We are here dealing with an international jurisdiction, not with national jurisdiction. Some states may be more ready to entrust such questions to an international tribunal, although the progress of the United Nations studies of an international criminal jurisdiction does not suggest much general acceptance of the proposal. The matter has relevance here because it shows the beginnings of an acceptance of the proposition that even in regard to matters wholly internal or domestic the sovereign state is not absolute master in its own house. Granted that its loss of mastery depends upon its consent, yet the adoption of many new legal standards to comport with the changing mores of the times depends

38. *Council of Europe News,* October 1955, p. 3 and Suppl. of August 1955. The commission continued its sessions December 15; *Council of Europe News,* January 1956, p. 4.

upon persuading some group or groups to give consent. In the United States the Congress must consent before there is a Child Labor Law, and the Senate must consent before the United States becomes bound by an international labor convention or an international human rights convention. In both instances the consent follows a conviction on the part of a sufficiently influential group that the proposed new rule is desirable. To put the still more obvious case, it is asserted that the United States cannot be hailed before an international tribunal without its consent. This is true, but it is equally true that the United States could not be sued in its own courts until Congress had given its consent, as through the passage of the Tucker Act. It does not help us to understand the general problem, therefore, to keep insisting upon the absoluteness of sovereignty and to emphasize, as Marshall did in the *Schooner Exchange,* that all exceptions "must be traced up to the consent of the nation itself." Marshall was forced to proceed at once to say that the consent "may be either expressed or implied," and as soon as one wanders into the field of implied consent one is off in the fictional realm again. One strains at the gnat of theoretical qualification of sovereignty and swallows the camel of actual limitation.

Two other theories of jurisdiction embodied in the laws of a number of states should be mentioned. One is the so-called passive personality theory illustrated by Article 6 of the Turkish Penal Code which was involved but not passed upon in the famous *Lotus* case. The article provides in essence: "Any foreigner who . . . commits an offense abroad to the prejudice of Turkey or of a Turkish subject . . . shall be punished in accordance with the Turkish Penal Code provided that he is arrested in Turkey."[39] A like provision in Article 186 of the Mexican Penal Code was involved in another *cause célèbre*, the Cutting case, which aroused the violent protests of the United States although actually the criminal libel, which was the basis of the prosecution in that case, seems to have circulated in Mexico and would thus have justified criminal proceedings on the basis of the objective territorial principle.[40]

The passive personality theory, which has been vigorously attacked, may be considered a limited application of the principle of universality.[41] This latter principle, recognized in the Corpus Juris Civilis, applied in medieval times, and found in many modern codes, is said to be justified by the solidarity of states in their struggle against the criminal.[42] In most codes the provisions for universal jurisdiction are hedged with numerous safeguards, such as lack of punishment elsewhere, lack of a demand for extradition, or re-

39. P.C.I.J., ser. A, no. 10 (1927), pp. 14–15. For other examples see Harvard Research, p. 578.

40. See para. 10 of the decision of the Bravos District Court in Briggs, *The Law of Nations*, p. 574. The United States with some justification contended that the decision was actually based on Article 186 of the Penal Code and took its stand in opposition to that provision supported by John Bassett Moore's classic opinion "Report on Extraterritorial Crime and the Cutting Case," *Foreign Rel. U.S.* (1887), p. 757. Judge Moore returned to the attack in his separate opinion in *The Lotus* case.

41. Harvard Research, p. 578.

42. See generally Harvard Research, comment on Article 10, pp. 573ff.

fusal of an offer to surrender the prisoner to some state having a claim to jurisdiction on one of the more usual grounds. The Harvard Research quotes the quaint instance from colonial New England: "It is enacted by the Court that whosoever haveing committed uncleanes in another Collonie and shall come hither and have not satisfyed the law where the fact was committed they shalbe sent backe or heer punished according to the nature of the crime as if the acte had bine heer done."[43]

If every state in the world had complete confidence in the administration of criminal justice in every other state, there could be little objection to the universal theory, leaving aside problems of evidence, which as we have seen are disregarded in many extensions of even the territorial theory. Unfortunately such confidence is lacking. The furor over the conclusion of the NATO Status of Forces Agreement and similar agreements with other countries, providing for the local trial of members of American armed forces stationed abroad in case of certain criminal offenses, is ample proof of this. Horrid specters were evoked of American GI's having their ears or hands cut off according to the imagined standards of punishment inflicted in some of our benighted allied countries. To still the clamor, American GI prisoners in Japan are incarcerated in a special jail where their accommodations are more ritzy than those available to the less fortunate Japanese citizen who violates the law. Those GI prisoners who have to be accommodated in another

43. *Ibid.*, p. 583.

prison, which does not have central heat, are provided by their jailers with hot water bottles.[44]

The long history of diplomatic claims for injuries to citizens abroad also bears testimony to the fact that jails are frequently places of abode which would not be selected by the most fastidious.[45] We are constantly being shocked by disclosures of crowded, unsanitary, and otherwise disgraceful conditions in the penal institutions and "snake-pits" of our own country. But whether or not our British and Canadian friends, for example, might be unwilling to have their citizens tried and punished in the United States—and our subversion cases have indeed given them pause—we are certainly unwilling to concede that an American citizen may be so dealt with in any land where he may happen to be, for offenses committed in the United States. The reaction is natural, and we can support our objections by various theoretical arguments against principles of unlimited universal jurisdiction. But of course we cannot raise any legal objection to any foreign state's asserting and exercising criminal jurisdiction over an American citizen who violates the local criminal law while in that state. All we can do is to aid him, insofar as possible, through consular or diplomatic interposition, and perhaps after the event press a diplomatic claim if his trial and punishment do not conform to the hypothetical international standard of justice which international claims commissions so frequently invoke.

44. Testimony of General Hickman before a subcommittee of the Senate Armed Services Committee, February 9, 1956.

45. See, for instance, the description in the Roberts Claim, United States *v.* Mexico (1926), Briggs, p. 551.

If the international community had progressed to the point of solidarity in a common struggle against the criminal, if it had also developed a unified conception of what is criminal, and if trial procedures were uniformly fair, many problems would be solved or would not even arise. A certain amount of such solidarity has developed, particularly over the last one hundred years in regard to such activities as piracy, the Negro slave trade, the narcotics traffic, and traffic in obscene publications and in women and children. But when Woodrow Wilson suggested at the Versailles Peace Conference that this last problem should be included in the objectives of the League of Nations, it is reported that Clemenceau commented aside: "Quel homme! Il a réformé le monde et maintenant il veut réformer le demi monde." The United Nations' efforts to secure agreement upon a code of offenses against the peace and security of mankind have met with small success. Differences in social customs and standards prevent a unified world view on the criminality of bigamy, or the sale and consumption of alcohol, or the smoking of opium; what is justifiable homicide in one country may be murder in another.

It would lead us still further from our present purpose to discuss here the possibility of treaty agreement on procedural safeguards surrounding the trial of any criminal, although the conclusion of such agreements, as is true of existing extradition treaties, would aid in the solution of some jurisdictional issues. For our present purposes the importance of these elements of the broad problem is that they serve to emphasize some of the real as distinguished from the theoretical aspects of jurisdiction.

On the basis of what has already been said the following conclusions emerge. The power element in jurisdiction amounts only to this, namely the possibility that the state's action will be effective. This condition is satisfied whenever the person charged with crime is physically within the custody of the court. It may also be said to be satisfied if the person charged is not physically present but has property within the state. So in the Blackmer case Mr. Blackmer was abroad, but a fine of $60,000 was satisfied by the attachment of his property within the United States.[46]

In the practice of a Nazi or Communist regime the power requirement may be satisfied when the accused is physically absent from the country, has no property therein, but does have there relatives who may be made to suffer for his alleged offense. This power is sufficiently well recognized to constitute a test of a person's employability by the United States Government, although here we get into an area in which reasonableness has played small part.

The reason why some such control over the person, his property, or his relatives is generally a prerequisite to the effectiveness of an exercise of jurisdiction is that the law-enforcing agents of a state may not exercise their authority within the confines of another state. Upon this proposition there is general agreement in both doctrine and practice to the extent that the habit of conduct is properly described as a rule of international law. Unless a state decides to resort to war, the restraint is actual in a case of two states of relatively substantial power. In a case involving a Great Power and a

46. Blackmer *v.* United States, 284 U.S. 421 (1932).

weak state, the decision maker of today generally seems to conclude that it is more advantageous to follow the rule, even in the case of a state with a predilection for aggression, since it is likely to have larger fish to fry and prefers to bide its time before arousing opposition. The existence of the rule is merely strengthened by the traditional exceptions which formerly justified such means of self-help as the landing of marines or other uses of force which are now expressly forbidden by Article 2(4) of the Charter of the United Nations.[47] The rule is perhaps also proved by the exceptional cases of exercise of official authority abroad, as when a consular officer performs official acts in a foreign country, or—in the type of case which writers love to mention—if President Eisenhower had signed an executive order or a commission in Geneva while attending the "Conference at the Summit."

Surely then one would agree that "If there was no jurisdiction in the nation to make the original seizure or arrest, there should be no jurisdiction in the court to subject [the person seized] to the nation's law." This statement by Dickinson, Reporter for the Harvard Research Draft on "Jurisdiction with Respect to Crime," he admits, expresses the desirable not the actual state of affairs.[48] The courts of the United States sustain this rule if the seizure is in violation of a treaty,[49] but not if it violates a general rule of customary

47. See Jessup, *A Modern Law of Nations,* ch. 7, "The Legal Regulation of the Use of Force."

48. Harvard Research, see comment on Article 16 and especially p. 631.

49. Cook *v.* United States, 228 U.S. 102 (1933).

international law. Under the American decisions, if the crime has been committed within the jurisdiction and the accused escapes, let us say to Canada or Mexico, and if he is unlawfully kidnaped or abducted in that foreign country and brought back into the United States, the court here has jurisdiction. When one recalls the extreme cases of constructive presence invoked to justify jurisdiction on what is called the territorial principle, it is clear that this rule is utterly inconsistent with the basic theories which are solemnly pronounced by the courts. Thus if X, a person who has never been in the United States but has always lived in Toronto, mails a swindling letter to someone in Detroit, and if the aggrieved Detroiter with some of his friends steals across the border and kidnaps X and forcibly brings him to Detroit, our courts would have jurisdiction to try X. And they would base their jurisdiction on the territorial principle! Canada might protest, and as the court said in the Lopez case, this would raise "serious questions, involving the claimed violation of its sovereignty, which may well be presented to the Executive Department of the United States, but of which this court has no jurisdiction."[50] If one is looking for a limitation on jurisdictional power one should seek it in what we may call a balance of power, which it has been found appropriate and convenient to establish among the states of the world. That the limitation does not flow from such concepts as territoriality or personality or nationality or interest, *per se*, is shown by the fact that any

50. *Ex parte* Lopez, 6 F. Supp. 342, 344 (S.D. Tex. 1934). Cf. Harvard Research, p. 629.

nation is free, if it so desires, to exercise jurisdiction over a stateless person in *terra nullius*.

To be sure, physical custody of the accused satisfies the criterion of effectiveness. But effectiveness is not a universal criterion of jurisdiction, as is seen in the provisions of many penal codes which provide for the trial, even of aliens, *in absentia* or *par contumace*. Judgments so rendered may indeed have a kind of potential effectiveness in the sense that they may prevent the person convicted from entering that state in the future. But surely this kind of effectiveness is very different from the power with which Holmes equated jurisdiction.

Moreover, the effectiveness which we usually associate with the exercise of territorial jurisdiction may be wholly lacking in the case of a government in exile; its potential effectiveness depends upon the hazard of war. We may say of the governments of The Netherlands and of Norway, for example, when they were functioning in England during World War II, that their territorial supremacy was only momentarily in abeyance. There were fewer governmental authorities indeed who were prepared to say the same of the Emperor Hailie Selassie in the winter of 1939. How do we know today whether the sovereignty of the Baltic states of Estonia, Latvia, and Lithuania is actually represented by their recognized diplomatic missions in Washington, or whether it has been permanently extinguished? The recent study by Marek tries to supply criteria for juridical answers to such questions, but at times one feels inevitably relegated to the land of hopes and cold war politics.[51]

51. Marek, *Identity and Continuity of States in Public International Law*.

Up to this point we have been considering penal or criminal jurisdiction. We have already noted that there is a tendency among writers to leave questions of jurisdiction in civil matters to the realm of conflict of laws or private international law. It seems to be true that there are very few instances in which foreign offices have made diplomatic complaints that a rule of the conflict of laws has been violated to the prejudice of their citizens, except perhaps where the conflicts rule has been embodied in a treaty as is the common practice of the Latin American and European countries. In such cases the complaint would be that the treaty was breached, which is customarily treated as a matter for intergovernmental protest within the realm of public international law. It is true that the Supreme Court in Hilton *v.* Guyot said that international law "in its widest and most comprehensive sense" includes the conflict of laws,[52] and the Austrian courts take the same position.[53] It is also true that writers have found it difficult to sort out the conflict of law and the public international law aspects of cases involving the enforcement of foreign judgments, especially in the plethora of cases which raise the problem of the effect of recognition or nonrecognition.[54] The *Restatement of Conflict of Laws* mentions international law as a possible limita-

52. 159 U.S. 113, 163 (1895).

53. Ignaz Seidl-Hohenveldern, "Relation of International Law to Internal Law in Austria," 49 *American Journal of International Law* 451, 454 (1955).

54. John R. Stevenson has done it well in "Effect of Recognition on the Application of Private International Law Norms," 51 *Columbia Law Review* 710 (1951) and in "The Relationship of Private International Law to Public International Law," 52 *ibid.* 561 (1952).

tion upon jurisdiction in some cases but does not attempt
to explore what Judge Hutcheson called "a new wonderland
of law."[55]

From the standpoint of considering transnational law
there seems to be little reason for attempting to distinguish
between civil and criminal cases in determining jurisdiction.
Is governmental interest less in civil cases than it is in criminal cases when its citizen abroad is affected? There is some
evidence that this is the case, but it is hard to find a satisfactory rationale. The history of the diplomatic protection
of citizens abroad is full of cases in which governments have
taken up the cudgels on behalf of citizens arrested and tried
for breach of the criminal laws of another country, but it is
the well-settled rule of the United States Department of
State that it will not interpose diplomatically in ordinary
contract claims. Special provisions in a claims convention
giving an international tribunal power to pass on contractual
claims of citizens of one state against the government of
another state are hardly an exception. But if a citizen's
property is taken by another state under a nationalization
program or otherwise, his government may come to his
defense if he does not receive adequate compensation.

In the transnational cases which are usually taken up
diplomatically and which therefore become truly international, the common element is generally the fact that a
private citizen of one country is in controversy with the
government of another country. All cases of criminal prose-

55. Claim of Ryan Trustee *v*. United States (1937), 32 *American Journal
of International Law* 593, 613 (1938).

cution, for example, have this element which is missing in a civil suit in contract or tort brought by one private person against another private person,[56] although the suit may abound in transnational complications. But the agency of the state whose jurisdiction comes in question is generally or at least frequently a court, and a court is involved whether the proceeding be civil or criminal. There is no reason why international law should be concerned with a court's jurisdiction when the proceeding ends in imprisonment for theft, but be unconcerned when it ends in imprisonment for debt involving fraud or willful disobedience of court orders as was still possible after the reform of the debt laws in England. Radin points out that the fraud required in these cases "is usually far short of the penal offense of that name," but that in 1905 over 11,000 debtors were imprisoned in England and as many as 2,875 even in 1927.[57] Should there be a different jurisdictional rule for the criminal and for the civil proceedings under the Sherman Antitrust Act where the case involves transnational elements?

Leaving aside the procedural requirements of constitutional due process, we find in the *Restatement of Conflict of Laws,* which is mainly concerned with civil and not criminal questions, that "The exercise of jurisdiction by a state through its courts over an individual may be based upon any of the following circumstances," five such then being listed. Let us consider them individually.

56. But it does exist in the case of a contract between an individual alien and the government.

57. Max Radin, article on "Debt" in *Encyclopaedia of the Social Sciences* (1935), 5, 37.

"(a) the individual is personally present within the state."[58] As we have seen, the presence of the person is usually required but is not generally considered by itself a reasonable basis for criminal jurisdiction. In criminal cases one looks further to ascertain the nature of the crime and where it was committed. In the civil case one does not care whether the contract, for example, was concluded in another country between aliens and related to matters to be performed in that country, if only the defendant is before the court. The *Restatement* refrains from expressing an opinion on the question that would be raised if the Toronto swindler in our hypothetical case were also sued in a civil action after having been forcibly brought to Detroit.[59]

Turn to the second basis of civil jurisdiction: "(b) [the individual] has his domicile within the state."[60] We have seen that the assertion of criminal jurisdiction based solely on domicile is made by some states but is by no means general. One should repeat that in the civil cases now under discussion there are of course requirements under the law of the United States concerning service of process which are not generally applicable in criminal cases. Under the Walsh Act, however, Blackmer was served, as the statute required, by an American consul in France with a subpoena requiring him to appear as a witness on behalf of the United States in a criminal trial. The offense charged was contempt of court in failing to comply with the subpoena. Although as noted

58. *Restatement,* p. 115.
59. See the Caveat, *ibid.,* p. 117.
60. *Ibid.,* p. 115.

the codes of a few states permit criminal prosecution *in absentia,* the Harvard Research was unable to find any case where an alien had been prosecuted who had not been taken into custody.[61] Domicile may also be a fictitious claim where it is not based on physical reality but on "operation of law."[62]

The third basis of civil jurisdiction is nationality, which is generally not utilized in United States law save in cases like those under the Walsh Act noted above. It is, however, commonly used in other states, and the *Restatement* notes that a foreign judgment of a court whose jurisdiction was based on the defendant's nationality may be given effect here so far as the basic jurisdictional requirement is concerned. The right to found criminal jurisdiction on the basis of nationality is of course generally recognized.

The fourth basis of civil jurisdiction is consent, which has no equivalent in criminal jurisdiction, except as one might imagine a repentant criminal going to a state which adopts the principle of universal jurisdiction and there surrendering himself to the authorities. If a conscience-smitten Frenchman who had committed a theft in France surrendered himself to the New York police and asked to be tried, the most that the United States authorities could do would be to ask the French Government if it wished to request his extradition. In civil cases, on the other hand, the consent to the jurisdiction when clearly proved removes any jurisdictional obstacle. Yet if one moves again to the truly international field,

61. Harvard Research, p. 600.
62. *Restatement,* pp. 50ff.

one finds that an alien's own government may not consider conclusive the alien's consent to the exclusive jurisdiction of the national courts of a state with whose government he makes a contract containing a familiar Calvo Clause.[63]

The fifth and final basis of civil jurisdiction is that the individual "has by acts done by him within the state subjected himself to its jurisdiction." For present purposes it is unnecessary to consider the constitutional questions raised in the United States relative to this basis of jurisdiction, nor the problem of defining what constitutes "doing business" especially by a foreign corporation. The concept is basically similar to that of the territorial theory in criminal law, where an act performed within the state is sufficient to base jurisdiction. One of the *Restatement's* illustrations, however, points to an important difference. "A statute of State X provides that in an action growing out of the operation of an automobile within the State by a non-resident, service of process may be made upon a public official, who shall forward a copy of the process by mail to the non-resident. A, a resident of State Y, operates an automobile in X and runs into and injures B. B brings an action in X against A, not otherwise subject to the jurisdiction of the State, and service of process is made in accordance with the statute. The court has jurisdiction to render a judgment against A." But had the accident resulted in B's death, our notions of criminal

63. For a recent comprehensive study of this controversial matter, see Donald R. Shea, *The Calvo Clause: A Problem of Inter-American and International Law and Diplomacy* (Minneapolis, University of Minnesota Press, 1955).

jurisdiction would not permit a criminal prosecution by X against A unless A were physically present in X. The distinction is deeply rooted in our legal concepts of the safeguards which should surround a person in a criminal case. Is the distinction one of general applicability to a state's jurisdiction in all transnational situations? Suppose that an act of A gives rise to a tort claim by B for damages which amount to $10,000 and is also a penal offense for which the penalty is a fine of $10,000. If B gets a judgment against A in State X in the manner described, the judgment may be sued on in Y and A's property may be attached to satisfy the debt. But if the law of X permitted a conviction of A *in absentia* and the fine were levied, Y would not permit X to collect it by proceeding against A's property in Y, because of the standard rule that one state will not aid another in the enforcement of its penal, revenue, or political laws.[64]

The purpose here is to test certain conclusions by sample situations and no pretense is made to completeness. Thus it is unnecessary to continue with an exploration of other bases of jurisdiction such as that involved in quasi-in-rem procedures against the attached property of nonresidents. Suffice it to note in this connection that in Switzerland a suit in personam can be brought against an individual having no domicile but having property, however little, in that country; the procedure is not quasi-in-rem, and in the eyes of American courts the Swiss court in such a case would not

---

64. Subject to treaties on judicial assistance in the case of fiscal laws, for example, see Briggs, p. 413.

be considered to have jurisdiction.[65] Yet Swiss law could hardly be called barbaric or unreasonable.

Just as the line between the international and the national should be questioned as a basis for legal classification, so should the standard distinction between criminal and civil. The fundamental question is to determine which national authorities may deal effectively with which transnational situations—effectively in the sense that authorities of other states will recognize that the exercise of authority is reasonable and will therefore give effect to judgments rendered or refrain from protests through the diplomatic channel. The old traditional bases of territoriality, nationality, and the like were well grounded historically but have developed beyond the boundaries of their historic justifications largely through the use of legal fictions. "Legal fiction," wrote Morris Cohen, "is the mask that progress must wear to pass the faithful but blear-eyed watchers of our ancient legal treasures. But though legal fictions are useful in thus mitigating or absorbing the shock of innovation, they work havoc in the form of intellectual confusion." "In English law," said Bentham still more vigorously, "fiction is a syphilis which runs in every vein and carries into every part of the system the principle of rottenness."[66]

---

65. Arthur Nussbaum, *American–Swiss Private International Law*, "Bilateral Studies in Private International Law," no. 1 (New York, Parker School of Foreign and Comparative Law, Columbia University, 1951), p. 31.
66. As quoted in my discussion of legal fictions in "International Law in the Post-War World," *Proceedings of the American Society of International Law* (1942), pp. 46, 50, 48.

It would be the function of transnational law to reshuffle the cases and to deal out jurisdiction in the manner most conducive to the needs and convenience of all members of the international community. The fundamental approach would not start with sovereignty or power but from the premise that jurisdiction is essentially a matter of procedure which could be amicably arranged among the nations of the world.[67] The transnational lawyer might bear in mind that even a genuine and not fictional territorial base is at times unsatisfactory, as in certain maritime situations: the problems raised by the enforcement of the United States Prohibition laws along Rum Row were not solved by a redefinition of territorial waters, but by international agreement on the procedures to be followed in apprehending foreign smugglers on the high seas.

67. In any expansion of this suggestion, one would of course need again to find an escape from one of the old semantic morasses, in this case the distinction between "substance" and "procedure." See e.g. Walter W. Cook, " 'Substance' and 'Procedure' in the Conflict of Laws," 42 *Yale Law Journal* 333 (1933); H. L. McClintock, "Distinguishing Substance and Procedure in the Conflict of Laws," 78 *University of Pennsylvania Law Review* 933 (1930).

3. THE CHOICE OF LAW
GOVERNING THE PROBLEMS

THE EXISTENCE OF JURISDICTION is often made to appear to flow from some immutable rule, but the exercise of jurisdiction may be recognized to be a matter of discretion; *forum non conveniens*. The international lawyer may think of the problem of jurisdiction over disputes concerning the internal management of a foreign vessel in port; the conflicts lawyer may consider the cases where courts decline to interfere in the internal management of a foreign corporation. In one case the ship, in the other the corporation, may be within the jurisdiction of the court, but the factual situation may be one in which the court decides it is preferable for it not to act. If the court does act international or transnational complications may result. Thus the Supreme Court of the United States held that it was a violation of the Volstead Act for an Italian ship to bring wine into port, even when the supply was sealed in its ship's stores, although the Italian law required the ship to serve wine as part of the crew's ration.[1] The master of a Swedish ship in the port of Philadelphia was held guilty of contempt for putting a seaman in irons on his return from court where he had filed

1. Cunard S.S. Co. *v.* Mellon, 262 U.S. 100 (1923). For the protests of the Italian and other governments, see Philip C. Jessup, *The Law of Territorial Waters and Maritime Jurisdiction* (New York, G. A. Jennings Co., 1927), pp. 222ff.

suit to recover his wages and for discharge, although the law of Sweden prohibited the master from recognizing the jurisdiction of a foreign court over any dispute between master and seaman.[2] A District Court in an antitrust proceeding ordered a British corporation, Imperial Chemical Industries, Ltd., to cancel an agreement with the American DuPont Company and reconvey to DuPont certain assigned patent rights. Another English company, Nylon Spinners, Ltd., which held an exclusive license from ICI for the use of the same patents and which was not a party to the antitrust case, sought an injunction from a British court to restrain ICI from complying with the United States court's order. The British Court of Appeals declined to be fettered by the American court's order, especially because that order provided that it should not operate against ICI for "action [taken] in compliance with any law . . . of any foreign government or instrumentality thereof to which ICI is at the time being subject and concerning matters over which under the law of the United States such foreign government or instrumentality thereof has jurisdiction."[3] The Master of the Rolls, with a polite bow to the District Courts of the United States, questioned whether the order did not "assert an extraterritorial jurisdiction which the Courts of this country [United Kingdom] can not recognize," notwithstanding comity.

2. *The St. Oloff*, 29 Fed. Cas. 591, no. 17, 735 (D. Pa. 1790).

3. See British Nylon Spinners Ltd. *v*. Imperial Chemical Industries Ltd. [1953] 1 ch. 19, 24, n. 4. Cf. the terms of the decree in United State *v*. General Electric Co., 115 F. Supp. 835 (D. N.J. 1953).

The same United States District Court refused to issue a judgment restraining a Canadian corporation from using a certain trademark in Canada, saying that "such an attempted exercise of jurisdiction might provoke justified resentment." But in regard to other matters in the complaint the court asserted its jurisdiction over the same Canadian corporation which had an office in New York. The court recalled the following events: "In 1947, subpoenas were issued out of this Court to some fifty Canadian pulp and paper companies, in the course of a Sherman Act investigation, requiring them to produce records before a grand jury in New York. The Ontario Parliament believed that this was an infringement upon the sovereignty of the Province and as a result, there was passed 'The Business Records Protection Act,' Revised Statutes of Ontario, 1950, Chap. 44, which prohibits any person in that Province from sending from Ontario to a point outside of Ontario any books, records, or other papers in response to any 'order, direction or subpoena of any legislative, administrative, or judicial authority in any jurisdiction outside of Ontario.' The statement in the Ontario Parliament by the Premier of Ontario on October 27, 1947 reflected the resentment against what the Premier called an attempt by the judicial authorities of the United States 'to invade the territorial integrity of Canada' by the issuance of these subpoenas requiring the production of records from Canadian companies relating to business done in Canada. He stated at the conclusion of his remarks to the legislature: 'I recognize that in population Ontario is a very small jurisdiction compared with that of the United States. Nevertheless, I trust no citizen of the United States will forget that Canadians are just as proud of their own nationality and just as jealous of their own sovereignty as is any citizen of their own country.' "[4]

The reaction of authorities in Switzerland has been similar to that of Ontario, and they have prevented under the Swiss Penal Code and Swiss Bank Law the production of papers which an American court ordered a plaintiff to produce. But again there was a disavowal in the American court of any thought that a party could be punished for contempt when noncompliance was required by a foreign authority.[5]

These few examples are not cited in any attempt to portray current American theories of jurisdiction over foreign corporations, or as a study of the extraterritorial application of the antitrust laws.[6] They are cited as illustrations of some of the problems which arise under present theories of jurisdiction applied to transnational situations. It has been suggested above that jurisdictional problems should be regarded

4. Vanity Fair Mills *v.* T. Eaton Co., 133 F. Supp. 522, 529, n. 2 (S.D. N.Y. 1955).

5. Von Opel *v.* Uebersee Finanz Korporation, 225 F. 2d 530 (D.C. Cir. 1955).

6. See George W. Haight, "International Law and Extraterritorial Application of the Antitrust Laws," 63 *Yale Law Journal* 639 (1954); William D. Whitney, "Sources of Conflict between International Law and the Antitrust Laws," *ibid.*, 655; Wilhelm Wengler, "Laws concerning Unfair Competition and the Conflict of Laws," 4 *American Journal of Comparative Law* 167 (1955), brings out many interesting points relevant to the ideas discussed here, including consideration of situations in which acts are both civil and criminal wrongs. See also Kenneth S. Carlston, "Antitrust Policy Abroad," 49 *Northwestern University Law Review* 569, 713 (1954–55).

as primarily procedural and not from the standpoint of sovereignty and power. The above examples point to the fact that even where power is thought to exist, the court may in its discretion decide not to exercise it. To be sure, in some matters such as that of regulating the practices of international cartels and combines, deep substantive cleavages separate national views as to what conduct is proper and what should be condemned. In such situations it is vitally important for the managers of the business to know whether they will come under the jurisdiction of, say, the United States or Switzerland. For this reason international cartels are apt to rely on economic power rather than legal sanction.[7] In other situations the difficulties may be due to the fact that the courts have certain ingrained notions of sovereignty or territoriality and certain suspicions and fears about the courts of other countries. In the United States we even consider that the "corporation at one end of the Hudson Tube is a 'foreign corporation' at the other end, and is there governed by 'foreign law.' "[8] In such cases a more rational approach to the problem of choice of law could be adopted. Obviously, in many cases two or more states may lay just claim to have such contacts with the factual situation as to justify both or all in asserting that they have jurisdiction to deal with the case. If one envisages the issue arising in some third disinterested and impartial jurisdiction, the merits of

7. Wolfgang Friedmann and P. Verloren van Themaat, "International Cartels and Combines" in *Anti-Trust Laws,* ed. Friedmann (Toronto, The Carswell Co., 1956), p. 481.

8. Whitney, p. 662.

the two claims might be weighed. By way of clarification and to get away from preoccupation with the rules obtaining in the courts of any one particular country on any given subject matter, it may be useful to consider certain *fora* where jurisdiction is not an issue, but where there is a problem of choice of law in the broad, nontechnical sense of that term.

An international court is established by means of a treaty or other form of agreement between or among states. The constituent agreement, or *compromis,* usually states what law the court shall apply.[9] Thus Article 38 of the Statute of the International Court of Justice says that the function of the court is to "decide in accordance with international law." The particularizations which follow in that Article indicate where the court may look for this law, namely in treaties, in custom, and in "the general principles of law recognized by civilized nations." As "subsidiary means for the determination of rules of law" the court is to utilize "judicial decisions and the teachings of the most highly qualified publicists of the various nations." If the parties agree, the court may decide *ex aequo et bono;* this is different from applying equity which it might find to be part of the "general principles of law," as Judge Hudson pointed out.[10] But an international court may be authorized to apply other law. For example, the special tribunal established by the

9. Manley O. Hudson, *International Tribunals—Past and Future* (Washington, Carnegie Endowment for International Peace and Brookings Institution, 1944), ch. 8.

10. In his separate opinion in The diversion of water from the Meuse case, P.C.I.J., ser. A/B, no. 70 (1937), p. 76.

United States and Canada to settle the Trail Smelter claims was directed to apply "the law and practice followed in dealing with cognate questions in the United States of America as well as International Law and Practice."[11] The tribunal apparently had a choice between the two designated bodies of law, but it did not find itself confronted with any conflict between them.

If the constituent instrument does not stipulate what law is to be applied the court is faced with a different situation. The Convention of 1890 establishing the Union of International Transport by Rail provided for an arbitral procedure by which the Central Office could give judgments in disputes arising between members of the Union. It is important to note that the members were railway administrations, some of them governmental and some of them private. It should also be noted that a governmental railway administration may be indistinguishable from the government itself.[12] Most of the cases were transnational, that is, involving administrations, public or private, of different countries. The Convention itself laid down some of the legal rules governing the rights of carriers and specifically said that the effects of the carrier's lien on goods transported would be governed by the law of the country in which delivery was made.[13]

11. U.S., *Treaty Series*, no. 893 (1935).

12. "All parties now agree that the Swedish State Railways . . . were part of the Swedish Government . . ." Dexter & Carpenter, Inc., *v.* Kunglig Jarnvagsstyrelsen, 43 F. 2d 705, 706 (2d Cir. 1930); cf. Mason *v.* Intercolonial Railway of Canada & Trustees, 197 Mass. 349 (1908).

13. See Articles 20–2 of the Convention in de Martens, *Nouveau Recueil Général de Traités*, ser. 2, vol. *19*, p. 306.

But aside from these brief references, neither the Convention nor the Rules of Procedure established by the Central Office indicated what law should be applied in the settlement of disputes. In 1890 it was not thinkable that international law could apply directly to a private company. In its first fifty years twenty-two disputes were referred to the Central Office for decision. In many cases the tribunal found the applicable rule of law in the Convention of 1890 or in other treaties. In one case between two state railways it was found unnecessary to decide whether German or Belgian law should be applied, since the general principle of responsibility for negligence was accepted by both laws. The respondent German administration was held negligent, but on equitable grounds the amount of the indemnity was reduced.[14] In a case where the applicant and one respondent were state railways and two other respondents were private companies, two respondents were found negligent and the proportion of fault was fixed on equitable grounds.[15] Where the Hungarian State Railways furnished improper cars to several state railways and one private railway company, all of whom joined as applicants, it was found impossible to

14. General Direction of the Belgian State Railways *v.* Direction of the Railways of the German Reich at Essen, case no. 20 (1922), 31 *Bulletin des transports internationaux par chemins de fer* (hereinafter cited as *Bulletin*) 1 (1923). The writer has drawn on Hudson and Sohn, "Fifty Years of Arbitration in the Union of International Transport by Rail," for these cases, with a memorandum prepared by Kersten Rogge, Harvard Law School.

15. General Direction of Italian State Railways *v.* South Railway Co. *et al.*, case no. 18 (1911), 19 *Bulletin* 221 (1911).

determine the extent of the damage due to this fact, and the proportion was determined *ex aequo et bono*.[16] In another case between Imperial General Direction of the Railways in Alsace and Lorraine (state railways) and Railway Company of the French Midi (a private company), there was a suit for payment of transportation charges which had been erroneously credited. The tribunal held the mistake in motives did not affect the validity of a contract under any of the civil laws which could be relevant, namely those of Switzerland, Germany, and France; the claim to invalidate the credit was dismissed.[17] In South German Frontier Railways (all state railways) *v.* Administrations of the Swiss Railway Association (all then being private railways although the Swiss Government was a stockholder), the claims related to the basis upon which compensation should be paid for the use by one railway of rolling stock belonging to another railway. There being no applicable contract or treaty provision, the tribunal applied the general principles of law and equity, basing its decision in particular on the principle that the loan of cars was an inherent part of international transportation, and that in consequence the lending administration should be reimbursed for its construction and maintenance expense.[18]

Attention has already been called to the stipulation of the

16. State Railways of Wuertemberg *et al. v.* State Railways of Hungary, case no. 17 (1909), 18 *Bulletin* 375 (1910).

17. Case no. 13 (1905), 13 *Bulletin* 332 (1905).

18. Case no. 4 (1897), 5 *Bulletin* 893 (1897).

applicable law in the Iranian oil settlement. Another case of
comparable nature is to be found in the Abu Dhabi arbitration. Here Sheikh Shakhbut of Abu Dhabi, one of the
Trucial states on the Persian Gulf, made an oil concession
contract with the Petroleum Development (Trucial Coast)
Ltd., which contained an arbitration clause under which
Lord Asquith of Bishopstone was ultimately called upon to
decide a dispute under the contract. Parts of his opinion are
worth quoting here:

"What is the 'Proper Law' applicable in construing this
contract? This is a contract made in Abu Dhabi and wholly
to be performed in that country. If any municipal system of
law were applicable, it would *prima facie* be that of Abu
Dhabi. But no such law can reasonably be said to exist. The
Sheikh administers a purely discretionary justice with the
assistance of the Koran; and it would be fanciful to suggest
that in this very primitive region there is any settled body
of legal principles applicable to the construction of modern
commercial instruments. Nor can I see any basis on which
the municipal law of England could apply. On the contrary
Clause 17 of the agreement . . . repels the notion that the
municipal law of any country, as such, could be appropriate.
The terms of that clause invite, indeed prescribe, the application of principles rooted in the good sense and common
practice of the generality of civilized nations—a sort of
'modern law of nature.' " Lord Asquith proceeded to state
that some of the rules of English law were "so firmly
grounded in reason" as to form part of this "modern law of
nature," while others which had been invoked were de-

velopments of peculiarly English history and were not applicable.[19]

In cases such as those just described there could be no question of invoking the rule *forum non conveniens;* but the tribunal might have invoked another rule, *lex non conveniens,* if such a rule existed, as perhaps it should.

A rule of *lex non conveniens* might well be applied, for instance, by the Administrative Tribunal of the United Nations if a plaintiff employee sought to have his contract of employment interpreted according to the law of New York or Switzerland, in either of which places it might have been signed and executed. The legal situations before this court present interesting features. It was established by resolution of the General Assembly of the United Nations, largely on the pattern of the similar tribunals of the League of Nations and of the International Labor Organization. The general function of the Tribunal is to decide controversies between persons employed in the Secretariat of the United Nations and the United Nations itself, represented by the Secretary-General. The parties, then, are a private person, an employee of the United Nations, as plaintiff or applicant and the international organization as defendant; this is the conclusion of the International Court of Justice, although Judges Hackworth and Levi Carneiro in their dissenting opinions asserted that it was only the Secretary-

19. In the Matter of an Arbitration between Petroleum Development (Trucial Coast) Ltd. and the Sheikh of Abu Dhabi. Award of Lord Asquith of Bishopstone, 1 *International and Comparative Law Quarterly* 247, 250–1 (1952).

General who is defendant.[20] The controversies are ones which arise out of the relations of employer and employee. It seems clear that it is correct to refer to those employment arrangements as "contracts" with both contractual and statutory elements. The Committee of Jurists, which advised the Secretary-General in 1952 concerning the difficult problem raised for him by loyalty investigations of American citizens so employed, had no doubt about the matter: "There can, we think, be no doubt that the rights of the staff in matters of their employment are contractual and that the terms of the contract are to be found in the Staff Regulations and the Rules promulgated as Staff Rules in pursuance of the regulations . . ."[21] The Statute of the Administrative Tribunal calls them contracts. So did the General Assembly in referring a question of the competence of the Tribunal to the International Court of Justice. The International Court, in its advisory opinion, refers to them and treats them throughout as contracts, and the three dissenting judges do not disagree with the majority on this point.

Now a contract is a legal conception. Contractual rights are legal rights. Legal rights must stem from some body of law. In the case of United Nations staff employment contracts what is that law? According to the International Court: "The contracts of service between the Organization and the staff members are contained in letters of appoint-

20. Effect of awards of compensation made by the U.N. Administrative Tribunal, Advisory Opinion of July 13th, 1954: I.C.J. Reports 1954, p. 47 at pp. 53, 81, 94.

21. UN Doc. A/INF/51, December 5, 1952, p. 35.

ment. Each appointment is made subject to terms and conditions provided in the Staff Regulations and Staff Rules . . ."[22] The Committee of Jurists had said that the terms of the contract are to be found in those regulations and rules. But neither the regulations nor the rules provide the answer to every disagreement which may arise under a contract any more than the statutory law provides an automatic rule of thumb for domestic courts in contractual litigation. To what law then does the Administrative Tribunal look for further guidance?

The author of the first standard book on the international civil servant, who is now a judge on the United Nations Administrative Tribunal,[23] maintained that it was "incontestable" that there is a contract between the individual employed and the international organization. But she concluded that while they are in a contractual situation, by virtue of the very object of their activity, they are subject to special rules which cannot be considered as being part of the corpus of private law, since one of the contracting parties has prerogatives governed and fortified by interstate public interest.[24] The rules of law applying between states are not of use and one must resort to the rules of internal public law, of administrative law, which present the most closely

---

22. I.C.J. Reports 1954, p. 57. In general, see also the Memorandum of the International Labour Organization submitted to the court in this case, I.C.J. *Pleadings, United Nations Administrative Tribunal,* p. 46.

23. Suzanne Basdevant (now Mme. Bastid), *Les fonctionnaires internationaux* (Paris, Recueil Sirey, 1931).

24. *Ibid.,* p. 85.

analogous situation.[25] She cites the Monod case before a special committee of three jurists appointed in 1925 by the Council of the League of Nations. There the Secretary-General terminated Monod's contract; he protested against this "unilateral breach." The jurists advised that it was not "uniquely a private law question," not a simple contract for services, but something "much more complex," being an arrangement for public employment. Therefore they thought it could not be judged merely according to the principles of private law and of civil laws, but according to the "principles of public law and of administrative laws."[26] They concluded however that Monod was entitled to an indemnity as a matter of right and not merely on equitable grounds, because once the exigencies of the public interest are satisfied it is necessary to take fair account of the private interests which have been injured.[27]

A legal committee of the League of Nations Assembly set up in 1932 said that the legal relationship between officials and the international organizations "is not a legal relationship of private law within the meaning of the civil law of any country," but under the League system "the official's right to his salary rest[s] upon a contract. If we have to do with a contract, it follows, under the general principles of law which are recognized by the Members of the League

25. *Ibid.*, p. 283.
26. *Ibid.*, pp. 79–80.
27. *Ibid.*, pp. 79–83. See also Hugh McKinnon Wood, "Legal Relations between Individuals and a World Organization of States," 30 *Grotius Society Transactions* 141, 148 (1944).

of Nations, that both parties are bound thereby, and that one party cannot alter the contract without the consent of the other party."[28]

During the Tenth General Assembly of the United Nations there were prolonged debates, especially in the Fifth Committee, on the proposal to provide for the review of the decisions of the Administrative Tribunal whose judgments under Article 10 of the original Statute "shall be final and without appeal." The United States fathered the proposal for review, having been defeated in its attempt to overturn by political decision the awards of a judicial body which had addressed itself to the judicial task of interpreting legal contracts instead of pronouncing political opinions in cases involving American citizens, members of the UN Secretariat, who had claimed the privilege of the Fifth Amendment in connection with United States security or loyalty procedures. The International Court of Justice had concluded that the tribunal was "established, not as an advisory organ or a mere subordinate committee of the General Assembly, but as an independent and truly judicial body pronouncing final judgments without appeal within the limited field of its functions."[29] In the course of the General Assembly consideration there was little indication that the delegates knew what law the Administrative Tribunal ap-

28. League of Nations, *Official Journal, Special Suppl.*, no. 107, pp. 206–7 (1932), discussed in Wood, pp. 150ff. See also the interesting discussion in the sixth meeting of the Finance Committee of the Twenty-First Assembly of the League of Nations, April 13, 1946, reproduced in Annex III to Memorandum of ILO, I.C.J. *Pleadings*, p. 84.

29. I.C.J. Reports 1954, p. 53.

plies. The Australian delegate, for example, said that "After a careful study of the Tribunal's judgments his delegation had been unable to ascertain what principles, if any, the Tribunal had followed in assessing the amount of compensation to be awarded."[30] The Belgian representative in the Fifth Committee thought that the Tribunal's "judicial principles were best developed in the light of experience."

In only one case has one of the international organizations' administrative tribunals applied the law of the place where the contract was made, or where it was to be performed, or the law of the nationality of the employee. *Lex non conveniens.* Obviously there is no "national" law of the UN or of the League of Nations or of any of the international organizations—aside from the rules and regulations which are part of the contract and the overriding constitutional base to be found in the Charter, Covenant, or other constitutional instrument. The Administrative Tribunal of the League used such expressions as these:

"The Tribunal . . . is bound to apply the internal law of the League of Nations, formulated either by a general statute, or by the decisions and texts which envisaged such specific cases, as well as the stipulations made between the Administration and its employees.

It is only in a case where there is no applicable positive law that the Tribunal would have occasion to rely on the general principles of law and equity."[31]

30. UN, General Assembly *Official Records,* Tenth Session, Fifth Committee, 500th Meeting, October 25, 1955, p. 75.

31. di Palma Castiglione *c.* Bureau International du Travail, League of Nations Administrative Tribunal, Judgment no. 1 (1929).

Again it said that since it was called upon "to decide according to the rules of law, it could not adhere to a thesis which finds no support in the positive dispositions of the Statute [of personnel] or in the general principles of law."[32]

Another case was decided in the light of "the principles governing the matter and admitted by doctrine and by various administrative jurisdictions." At another point in the same case it said that certain allegations did not conform "either to generally recognized principles or to the positive provisions of the Statute."[33] In another case it remarked that "there is no reason to derogate from the general principle of law that the costs . . . are paid by the losing party."[34] When this view was cited by the Administrative Tribunal of the United Nations,[35] the Legal Department of the United Nations Secretariat argued vigorously, with ample citation of national laws and the jurisprudence of international tribunals, that there was no such general principle of law.[36]

Until the dissolution of the League of Nations in 1946, the Administrative Tribunal of the League was available to

---

32. Souc *c.* Secrétariat de la Société des Nations, *ibid.*, Judgment no. 6 (1932).

33. Bouvaist-Hayes *c.* Secrétariat de la Société des Nations, *ibid.*, Judgment no. 4 (1930).

34. Schumann *c.* Secrétariat de la Société des Nations, *ibid.*, Judgment no. 13 (1934).

35. Aubert and fourteen others *v.* Secretary-General of the UN, Judgment no. 2 (1950), UN Doc. A/CN.5/Decisions/Cases 1–15/2, July 3, 1950.

36. UN Doc. A/CN.5/5, December 13, 1950.

officials of the International Labor Office; thereafter the Tribunal was taken over and maintained by the ILO. Its jurisdiction is now accepted by WHO, UNESCO, WMO, and FAO.[37] This Tribunal has made many awards *ex aequo et bono*.[38] One judgment shows a resort to the principles of conflict of laws and accordingly to national law which seems to be unique in the jurisprudence of such administrative tribunals.[39] The complainant was a clerk in the ILO Branch Office in Paris and was dismissed on the abolition of her position. The Tribunal flatly rejected the possibility of a judgment *non liquet* on the theory of the existence of a "gap" in the law. It said "that one of the fundamental tenets of all legal systems is that no court may refrain from giving judgment on the grounds that the law is silent or obscure." It then stated "that the circumstances show that the two parties seem to agree implicitly that the national legislation of the place in which the ILO Branch Office is situated should by analogy be applied in this case, and that the Director-General has himself stated that this is the procedure normally followed in all the Branch Offices." Accordingly it was necessary to enquire whether "French legislation has been respected in this case." On examining the French law the Tribunal concluded that it had not been sufficiently proved that the procedure of dismissal required by that law could have been applied in this case, but it proceeded to give judg-

---

37. UN Doc. A/2909, June 10, 1955, Annex II, p. 6.
38. E.g. in Judgments nos. 6, 17, 18, 22, 23, 24.
39. Degranges *v.* ILO, Judgment no. 11 (1953).

ment on the basis of the stipulations for compensation in such cases as provided in a French law of 1947. One may note that in current letters of appointment in the ILO the following language is used: "This letter of appointment . . . will, subject to the provisions of paragraph 5, constitute a contract governed by the general principles of law but will not create a contractual relationship subject in any respect to the law of any one country."

It should be noted also that the idea of an administrative tribunal to perform the functions described is derived principally from the French system of administrative law which is strange to American thinking. One notes this in the case of the UN Administrative Tribunal before the International Court of Justice, in the contrast between the dissenting opinion of Judge Levi Carneiro, a Brazilian who cites French sources, and that of Judge Hackworth, an American who talks in Anglo-American terms.[40] Actually the League of Nations realistically took this historical fact into account and staffed its Tribunal with Continental Europeans and never appointed an Anglo-Saxon judge. The same factors were largely responsible for the United States opposition to the UN Administrative Tribunal, both at the time of its establishment and in the later controversy over its decisions.

Judge Hackworth in his dissenting opinion said that contracts between the United Nations and "outside entities . . . such as contracts for the purchase of supplies and equipment,

40. Cf. Jacob M. Lashly, "Contrasting Approaches to the Employment Rights of the United Nations Staff Members," American Bar Association, Section of International and Comparative Law, *Proceedings* (1955), p. 19.

contracts for services, the lease of premises, etc. . . . are governed by private law concepts."[41] But contracts of employment between staff members and the Secretary-General, in his view, are not so governed but are governed "by provisions of the Charter, and by regulations made pursuant to the Charter." Disputes arising out of such contracts, he said, are "*intra*-organizational" or "of a domestic character." He did not suggest to what body of law the Tribunal should look in filling the gaps. According to the dissenting opinion of Judge Levi Carneiro, on the other hand, "The officials of the United Nations are bound by a 'public law contract,' "[42] whatever that may imply.

The UN Administrative Tribunal has relied on that convenient reservoir, the general principles of law. It has distinguished between contractual and statutory elements in the relations between the staff members and the Organization: "All matters being contractual which affect the personal status of each staff member e.g. nature of his contract, salary, grade;

"All matters being statutory which affect in general the organization of the international civil service, and the need for its proper functioning e.g., general rules that have no personal reference.

"While the contractual elements cannot be changed without the agreement of the two parties, the statutory elements on the other hand may always be changed at any time

---

41. I.C.J. Reports 1954, p. 82.
42. *Ibid.*, p. 95.

through regulations established by the General Assembly, and these changes are binding on staff members."[43]

Unlike the ILO Tribunal, the UN Administrative Tribunal has not based any one of its sixty-two judgments through December 1955 on the doctrine *ex aequo et bono,* although it has invoked equity. Neither has it followed the ILO Tribunal's resort to national law in the Desgranges case, although more than either of the other administrative tribunals, the UN Tribunal has relied on their jurisprudence and has frequently cited its own prior judgments. The Legal Department of the UN Secretariat has argued against the applicability of precedents drawn from the League of Nations Administrative Tribunal "in the same manner as the United Nations cannot be considered as the successor at law of the League of Nations." Moreover, it was argued that the principles of the League Tribunal's judgments could not even be applied by analogy, because of differences in the League and UN Statutes of the Tribunals and in the rules and conditions of employment of the two groups of personnel.[44] The Tribunal has not accepted this point of view in its subsequent judgments. The UN Administrative Tribunal has also cited decisions of the International Court of Justice, the Universal Declaration of Human Rights, and in one case McCormick, *Handbook on the Law of Damages.* It has

43. Kaplan *v.* Secretary-General of the UN, Judgment no. 19 (1953), UN Doc. AT/DEC/19, August 21, 1953.

44. Memorandum of the Legal Department in regard to the Competence of the Administrative Tribunal to Award Costs, UN Doc. A/CN.5/5, December 13, 1950.

also reflected the influence of its locale by referring to "due process" and to "implied powers in the United States constitutional law." On the other hand it has used the expression, the "integral law" of the United Nations, and has relied on "directives" of the Secretary-General and administrative practices of the UN.[45] It seems clear that a distinct body of international administrative law is gradually being established by this jurisprudence, and one finds that plaintiffs in their submissions to the Tribunal are constantly invoking it.

Under the resolution adopted by the General Assembly at its Tenth Session, the International Court of Justice may now be called upon by an established procedure to review judgments of the Administrative Tribunal. Irrespective of the advantages or disadvantages of this provision it is true, as the Legal Adviser of UNESCO pointed out, that such a practice "may encourage the progressive establishment of a unified jurisprudence in international administrative law . . . "[46] The Australian representative favored the legislative approach of amending the statute of the Administrative Tribunal to provide it with principles upon which to base its awards of damages.[47]

Here then we have judicial bodies interpreting contracts and awarding damages without being able to draw upon any specific body of law and, in general, without resorting to the rules of conflict of laws. They do draw upon general

45. See Judgments nos. 4, 56, 55, and 59.
46. UN Doc. A/2917/Add.1, August 15, 1955, p. 3.
47. UN Doc. A/2909, June 10, 1955, p. 23.

principles of law which may essentially be a good description of conflicts rules themselves.

International claims commissions have generally avoided the necessity of grappling with the problem faced by the administrative tribunals by relying on the traditional theory that the state is injured through the injury to its national and that therefore the claim is truly international, i.e. a claim of one state against another state. Under this fiction, rules of public international law are readily found to be applicable.[48] But the practice is not wholly uniform. Judge Parker as Presiding Commissioner in the German-American Mixed Claims Commission at the close of World War I, especially in establishing rules for the measurement of damages, drew freely upon the law of the United States and of Germany and found rules common to both the civil and the common law.[49] In the case of domestic commissions established to pass on international claims, provisions determining the applicable law differ. Currently the United States Foreign Claims Settlement Commission is to utilize "the applicable principles of international law, justice and equity." The British counterpart, the Foreign Compensation Commission, has to apply solely British national law as laid down in the governing Orders in Council, which, *inter alia,* determine the validity of certain transactions relating to property

---

48. See generally, Jessup, *A Modern Law of Nations,* ch. 5.

49. The Lusitania Cases (1923), Mixed Claims Commission, United States and Germany, *Administrative Decisions and Opinions of a General Nature and Opinions in Individual Lusitania Claims and Other Cases to June 30, 1925* (Washington, Government Printing Office, 1925), p. 17.

situated in a foreign state without any regard to the law of the situs where the property was transferred.[50]

In the Serbian Loans case the Permanent Court of International Justice was confronted with the necessity of interpreting loan contracts. "Any contract which is not a contract between States in their capacity as subjects of international law is based on the municipal law of some country," said the court[51] (but the court did not have in mind contracts of employment between a staff member and an international organization). Like any national court, the Permanent Court in this case fell back on conflict of laws or private international law to aid it in its choice of law. It noted that some rules of private international law are to be found in treaties and are thus transformed into "true international law"; other rules "may be common to several states," in which case, although the court did not say so, they might form part of the general principles of law. Apart from these two situations, the court said that the rules of private international law "form part of municipal law."

A special situation was presented in the Mixed Arbitral Tribunals established under the peace treaties at the end of World War I, because individuals were given direct access to these courts to press their claims against the former enemy states. Since the cases therefore were not international in the sense of being state *v.* state, public international law, or what

50. Alfred Drucker, "Compensation for Nationalized Property: The British Practice," 49 *American Journal of International Law* 477, 480, 485 (1955).

51. P.C.I.J., ser. A, nos. 20/21 (1929), p. 41.

the Permanent Court called true international law, was not considered generally applicable except for the purpose of interpreting the treaties. The Tribunals, therefore, while resorting in some cases to private international law and to national laws, frequently fell back on general principles of law and on equity. For example, in one case the German-Portuguese Tribunal said: ". . . in the absence of rules of international law applicable to the facts in litigation, the arbitrators ought to fill the gap by deciding according to the principles of equity while remaining with the spirit [*sens*] of international law applied by analogy, and in taking account of its evolution."[52]

Judges in national courts do not have the same freedom in determining what law to apply, but their process of making new case law is not fundamentally very different from the international judge's resort to the general principles of law, even though they label their source as the "wisdom of the founding fathers" or the "spirit of the constitution" or "the rule of reason." An American judge has some latitude in a choice of law although, to be sure, the Supreme Court of Errors of Connecticut could not disregard a Connecticut survival statute merely on the ground that it preferred some rule prevailing in Japan or Uruguay. We do not in general

52. Charles Carabiber, *Les jurisdictions internationales de droit privé* (Neuchatel, Éditions de la Baconnière, 1947), p. 258. See also Jean Teyssaire and Pierre de Solere, *Les tribunaux arbitraux mixtes* (Paris, Les Éditions internationales, 1931), pp. 149ff; Rudolf Blühdorn, "La fonctionnement et la jurisprudence des tribunaux arbitraux mixtes crées par les traités de Paris," The Hague Academy of International Law, 41 *Recueil des Cours* 194–5 (1932, III).

imitate the frankness of the provision in the Swiss Civil Code which provides in Article 1: "The Code applies to all legal questions for which it contains a provision in its term or its exposition. If no command can be taken from the statute, then the judge shall pronounce in accordance with the customary law, and failing that, according to the rule which he as a legislator would adopt. He should be guided therein by approved precept and tradition."[53] But an Act of Congress in 1860 is not very different in its provisions determining the law to be applied in United States consular courts. The provisions read in part as follows: "Jurisdiction . . . [is] exercised and enforced in conformity with the laws of the United States. . . . But in all cases where such laws are not adapted to the object, or are deficient in the provisions necessary to furnish suitable remedies, the common law and the law of equity and admiralty shall be extended in like manner over such citizens and others in those countries; and if neither the common law, nor the law of equity or admiralty, nor the statutes of the United States, furnish appropriate and sufficient remedies, the ministers in those countries, respectively, shall, by decrees and regulations which shall have the force of law, supply such defects and deficiencies."[54]

We have also explicitly authorized one of our courts to decide a case according to international law,[55] and there is

---

53. *The Swiss Civil Code,* tr. Robert P. Shick, Official Publication of the Comparative Law Bureau of the American Bar Association (Boston, The Boston Book Co., 1915), p. 1.

54. 22 U.S.C. sec. 145 (1952).

55. See Royal Holland Lloyd *v.* United States, 73 Ct. Cl. 722 (1931).

more liberality than formerly in allowing the parties to a contract to choose for themselves what law they wish to have govern their respective obligations.

Theoretically, at least, difficult questions of choice of law might occur in suits arising out of the nonperformance of contracts other than employment contracts, when one party is the United Nations or some other international organization. Suppose, for example, the United Nations contracts with an Italian firm to install in the United Nations headquarters in New York certain electrical equipment. The contract is signed by the company's agent and by the Secretary-General in the latter's office in the headquarters building. One might say that the contract was made and was to be performed "in the United Nations," and that in case of a dispute arising from alleged faulty installation the law of the United Nations should apply in interpreting the contract. But in this sense there is no United Nations law. It would be quite unrealistic to say that the fiction of extraterritoriality is outmoded, although this is true, and then to conclude that the law of New York should govern. If the contract also called for performance in United Nations headquarters in Geneva, would Swiss law be applicable to that part of the contract? Probably the Italian contractor in New York would rely on Article 3, section 7(b) of the Headquarters Agreement between the United States and the United Nations, which provides that "Except as otherwise provided in this agreement or in the General Convention, the federal, state and local law of the United States shall apply within the headquarters district."[56] But there is no equivalent provision in Switzerland. Perhaps the court would follow the suggestion of Professor Cavers and say that its choice of law "would not be the result of the automatic operation of a rule or principle of selection but of a search for a just decision in the principal case."[57] If the question at issue were the authority or capacity of the agent of the United Nations who signed the contract, this might well be resolved by United Nations law. It would be held, for instance, in the words of Judge Hackworth's dissenting opinion already cited, that the Secretary-General's "official acts . . . engage the responsibility of the Organization."[58]

Suppose again that a New York contractor agrees to install an elevator in the United Nations building and one of his employees is injured on the job by what New York law would consider the negligence of a United Nations employee. Suppose further that the United Nations had adopted regulations which would negative the idea of such negligence. Under the Headquarters Agreement the UN may "make regulations, operative within the headquarters district, for the purpose of establishing therein conditions in all respects necessary for the full execution of its functions. No federal, state or local law or regulation of the United States which is inconsistent with a regulation of the United

56. U.S., *T.I.A.S.* 1676 (1947).

57. David F. Cavers, "A Critique of the Choice-of-Law Problem," 47 *Harvard Law Review* 173, 193 (1933).

58. I.C.J. Reports 1954, p. 82.

50208

Nations authorized by this section shall, to the extent of such inconsistency, be applicable within the headquarters district."[59] Assuming the United Nations had waived its immunity, a New York or Federal court would presumably hold that it was not liable in an action for damages. Kelsen says such UN regulations "have the character of administrative law." He follows the traditional American conflicts point of view in adding: "In so far as they are to be applied by courts of the United States, they are American law whose creation is delegated by an international agreement entered into by the United States and the United Nations."[60]

The United Nations has saved the courts the trouble of examining some problems of this kind by adopting the practice of inserting in all contracts for supplies, etc., an arbitration clause which adopts the rules of the American Arbitration Association or of the International Chamber of Commerce; Specialized Agencies follow the same practice.[61] So did the League of Nations.[62] But this merely shifts the choice of law problem to another tribunal.

Strictly private law principles such as that of subrogation have also been invoked in drafting agreements between, for example, UNICEF and receiving governments, whereby

59. U.S., *T.I.A.S.* 1676 (1947), Art. 3, sec. 8.

60. Hans Kelsen, *The Law of the United Nations* (New York, F. A. Praeger, 1950), p. 351.

61. See the discussion by Jean-Flavien Lalive, "L'Immunité de juridiction des états et des organisations internationales," The Hague Academy of International Law, 84 *Recueil des Cours* 298ff. (1953, III).

62. Wood, p. 144; cf. Lalive, pp. 317–18, 325–6.

the latter assume responsibility for any claims asserted against the Fund or its agents arising from its operations in a receiving state. The UN has voluntarily utilized the New York State Workman's Compensation law procedures and is insured against injuries suffered by visitors to its buildings. No difficulty arises where there is such voluntary acceptance or invocation of some local law, but there is a problem where the UN stands on its position as an international organization.[63] It is quite possible that national courts would and should apply the acts of state doctrine to the United Nations and refuse to pass upon the validity of its relations with its employees, even where the Organization's immunity is waived or is deemed inapplicable.[64] As early as 1931 the Italian Court of Cassation recognized that Italian law could not govern a claim for compensation of an employee dismissed by the International Institute of Agriculture, saying: "The particular system of the Institute must be sufficient unto itself, both in regard to substantive rules and to rules governing the relations of its internal management, such as those concerning employment. The gaps in its substantive law are filled by means common to all autonomous legal systems, that is, by analogy and by assimilation, through a

63. In considering whether it is public or private law which applies to the United Nations and its specialized agencies, one may recall that the same question has been asked with regard to international cartels. Friedmann and van Themaat in *Anti-Trust Laws*, pp. 480ff.

64. Cf. the Mexican case referred to in Annual Report of the Secretary-General on the Work of the Organization, 1 July 1953—30 June 1954, General Assembly, *Official Records: Ninth Session, Suppl. No. 1*, UN Doc. A/2663 (1954), p. 105.

process of deduction, of the general or universal principles of law."[65]

The illustrations already evoked are perhaps sufficient to emphasize certain points.

1. There is nothing in the character of the parties which precludes the application of one or the other bodies of law into which the legal field is traditionally divided. The liability of a state for its actions may be governed by international law, by conflict of laws, by its own domestic law, or by foreign national law. The same is true of an international organization if we regard its constitution, statutes, and regulations as constituting its "domestic law." On the other hand, the liability of a corporation or of an individual may be determined by national law, foreign law, conflict of laws, or public international law.

2. There is nothing in the character of the forum which precludes it from applying one or the other of these bodies of law. A national court applies the law of its own country, the law of foreign countries, conflict of laws, and international law. International courts also apply international law, conflict of laws, and national law. In both cases, to be sure, the superior authority which creates the court or regulates the court's activities may specify what law it shall apply or not apply in given circumstances. Also the court may rationalize that it "makes its own," whatever law it applies.

3. There is no distinction between civil and criminal law in terms of its applicability to individuals, corporations, or

65. International Institute of Agriculture *v.* Profili, *Annual Digest of Public International Law Cases,* ed. Lauterpacht (1929–30), case no. 254.

states, again allowing for prescriptions laid down by the appropriate authority regarding the competence of a particular tribunal.

This last proposition may require some clarification. There is no doubt that criminal law is applied to corporations, but is there a criminal law which applies to states? While doctrine has generally avoided the conclusion that there is,[66] this result is based on the traditional deference to the idea of state sovereignty. For familiar reasons, at the close of World War II it was decided that the trial of war criminals should deal with individuals rather than states, but the basic theory was that aggressive war had become a crime which states might commit. The Genocide Convention provides for the trial of individuals. In the United Nations discussions of an international criminal jurisdiction and of a code of offenses against the peace and security of mankind, attention has been focused on the trial of individuals, but the idea of state guilt has not been excluded on theoretical grounds. The resolution of the General Assembly of the United Nations condemning the Communist regime in China for aggression in North Korea was a judgment that a criminal, not a civil offense under international law had been committed by a state. The resolution of the Security Council of January 19, 1956, condemning the Israeli attack on Syria[67] was likewise a criminal, not a civil judgment, although officials would never put it that way. It is outside the scope of this treatment to explore in detail the contro-

66. Cf. Jessup, *A Modern Law of Nations,* pp. 10ff.
67. UN Doc. S/3538, January 19, 1956.

versial question whether the principal organs of the United Nations do on occasion pronounce judgments which may be considered the exercise of a judicial function; it must suffice here to say that in my opinion they do.[68]

In less spectacular fields there are numerous cases in which international tribunals have rendered decisions which must be considered to be essentially criminal rather than civil, although for the reasons already suggested the tribunals are careful not to couch their judgments in that form. Let us use as a test the distinctions drawn by the United States Supreme Court in deciding whether a contempt is civil or criminal: Is the punishment wholly remedial, serving only the purpose of the complainant, or is it intended as a deterrent to offenses against the public? Here we must pause to emphasize that, aside from the trials of war criminals, the procedures of the international society in its present condition of still embryonic organization make it necessary to define the term "punishment" rather broadly to include condemnations and reprimands, as if there were a tacit understanding that the court was imposing, so to speak, a suspended sentence—suspended indefinitely until world organization is more highly developed. We may pass over the cases arising before the development of the United Nations where states, utilizing the then legal forms of self-help, forced offending states to pay what were in effect both compensatory and punitive damages.[69] If we look only at the decisions of international

68. Perhaps ECOSOC does not; see *United Nations: Repertory of Practice of United Nations Organs* (1955), vol. *3*, p. 260, par. 46.

69. See for example Jessup, *A Modern Law of Nations*, pp. 118ff.

tribunals we find numerous instances in which mixed claims commissions have awarded punitive damages, although the tendency is to avoid the use of the term. A clear case is presented by the award of the international tribunal to which the Canadian complaint against the United States in the *I'm Alone* case was submitted. The tribunal held that the action of the United States Coast Guard cutter in sinking the Canadian vessel was illegal; it awarded money damages to compensate the captain and crew of the *I'm Alone* and also required the United States to make an apology to Canada and to pay $25,000 "as a material amend in respect of the wrong."[70] In the Corfu Channel case the International Court of Justice held that the United Kingdom "violated the sovereignty of the People's Republic of Albania" but "that this declaration by the Court constitutes in itself appropriate satisfaction."[71] In the *Carthage* and *Manouba* cases before the Permanent Court of Arbitration, France asked for compensation for the damage to the vessels and for "one hundred thousand francs for the moral and political injury resulting from the failure to observe international common law and conventions binding both Italy and France." The court held that Italy's action was illegal and said that this holding "constitutes in itself a serious penalty."[72] It might be suggested that international law here, as elsewhere, retains certain primitive relics and that judgments of this kind are examples

---

70. *Ibid.*, p. 120.

71. Corfu Channel Case, Judgment of April 9th, 1949: I.C.J. Reports 1949, p. 4 at p. 36.

72. Jessup, *A Modern Law of Nations*, p. 40.

of the application of the theory of punishment by disgrace which has largely disappeared in the modern state[73] and which, one must concede, is quite as ineffective when applied in this manner to the state itself as was excommunication to Martin Luther or Henry VIII.

The point to be made is not the effectiveness or ineffectiveness of the procedures and organization of the international community but whether this traditional legal distinction between criminal and civil law poses itself as an imperative which must be heeded when one is considering what kind of law may be applicable to states. The answer to the question thus phrased is "no," although one may anticipate that for some time the characterization of state acts as criminal will be generally used only in conflict situations of tension and as a device for expressing the extreme reprobation with which the acts of some maverick government are regarded.

Transnational law then includes both civil and criminal aspects, it includes what we know as public and private international law, and it includes national law, both public and private. There is no inherent reason why a judicial tribunal, whether national or international, should not be authorized to choose from all of these bodies of law the rule considered to be most in conformity with reason and justice for the solution of any particular controversy. The choice need not be determined by territoriality, personality, nationality, domicile, jurisdiction, sovereignty, or any other rubric save as these labels are reasonable reflections of human

73. Cf. Hans von Hentig, article on "Punishment" in *Encyclopaedia of the Social Sciences* (1935), *12*, 714.

experience with the absolute and relative convenience of the law and of the forum—*lex conveniens* and *forum conveniens*.

But, it will be objected, one purpose of law is certainty. Individual persons, corporations, states, and international organizations must know the rules by which they should govern their conduct from day to day; such certainty cannot exist if decisions are to be rendered according to the whim of the judge who in his travels may have become fascinated by the tribal customs of Papua. The old customary law of Burma provided that if I entertain a guest at dinner who drinks well but not too wisely, and who on his way home is beaten by robbers or clawed by a tiger or bitten by a cobra, I am liable.[74] But we do not consider it reasonable to impose such liability on the exurbanite host whose homeward-bound guest is injured through one of the hazards of the environs of New York City. Clearly the law must be specified. By whom? By the authority which has the power to control the decisions of those who will sit in judgment. Such authority may be found in the Connecticut Legislature, in the Congress of the United States, or in the joint will of several states expressed through treaties or resolutions of the UN General Assembly. It may also be found in the courts themselves as when they rely on a Restatement of the American Law Institute to guide their choice of law where the controlling legislature has not prescribed the rule they must follow. The courts should have, in Judge Wyzanski's phrase, "the robust common sense to avoid writing opinions

74. E. Maung, *The Expansion of Burmese Law* (1951), p. 56.

and entering decrees adapted with academic nicety to the vagaries of forty-eight States,"[75] or, we may add here, of seventy-eight nations.

We are here dealing of course only with transnational situations. Much existing law has developed or has been enacted with an eye merely to the local or internal problem. Modern communications and contacts have made the transnational situations much more frequent and familiar; and actually a great deal of law has been created with the specific purpose of regulating such situations—rules regarding the enforcement of foreign judgments, arrangements for extradition, statutes and treaties governing acts on the high seas or in the air, regulation of double taxation, provisions determining inheritance by alien heirs, protection of trade marks and copyrights, and a multitude of other matters.

Where the law-making authority is national, the procedural problem of making new rules better suited to the regulation of transnational situations, that is, the creation of new transnational law, presents no difficulty. The difficulty lies—as the UNESCO Charter says of wars—in the minds of men. The minds of men are trained, or so we fondly believe, in our schools and universities. If those who are trained, particularly in our law schools and graduate schools of political science, are nourished on the pap of old dogmas and fictions, it is not to be expected that they will later approach the solution of transnational problems with open-minded

75. National Fruit Product Co. *v*. Dwinnel-Wright Co., 47 F. Supp. 499, 504 (D. Mass. 1942).

intelligence instead of open-mouthed surprise. Within the local or national framework education has made great strides in seeking to convey an appreciation of the economic, social, and political problems which the sciences of law and government seek to adjust. In the international or, more broadly, the transnational area there are occasional beacons which burn brightly but there are few well-lighted avenues.

The problem of developing transnational law is not actually so difficult as it is sometimes made to appear. Unquestionably much remains to be done in arousing an interest and creating an understanding of the nature and importance of transnational problems before much action will be taken by those having authority to provide wise rules for their solution. It may well be that a revaluation of the problem, for example, of "international combines and national sovereigns" would result, as Timberg suggests in his stimulating analysis, "in increased recourse to private municipal law as a method of irrigating the arid interstices that characterize so much of the potentially fertile acres of international commercial law."[76]

There are helpful precedents to guide the general process, especially from the development of maritime law which has been predominantly transnational since the days of the Phoenicians in the 14th century B.C. The law of general average, for example, which is traced at least to the Rhodian sea law of the 7th century B.C., has been codified by voluntary action of shipping interests through a process which

76. Timberg, "International Combines and National Sovereigns," p. 609.

received its initiative largely from the underwriters in 1860. A general nongovernmental maritime conference was convened to bring about uniformity in the various national applications of the law of general average. At first it was contemplated that uniformity should be obtained by the drafting of a bill which might be enacted into law in the legislatures of all maritime countries. This approach was superseded by the device of voluntary private agreement. Repeated nongovernmental maritime conferences, at which all interests and many countries were represented, finally agreed upon the York–Antwerp Rules which are today in common use throughout the world by virtue of the voluntary insertion in bills of lading and charter parties of a clause providing that all claims for general average are to be settled in conformity with the York–Antwerp Rules.[77]

On the other hand, the rules of the road at sea have become uniform through the adoption of identical legislation in many maritime states. The British took the lead, and their Merchant Shipping Amendment Act of 1862 "was accompanied by a set of 'Regulations for preventing collisions at sea,' which were adopted by the United States in 1864 and, in less than ten years, were accepted as obligatory by more than thirty of the maritime States of the world."[78]

77. See *Lowndes & Rudolf's Law of General Average and the York–Antwerp Rules* (8th ed. by Donaldson and Ellis, London, Stevens & Sons, 1955), pt. 2, for the history of the development.

78. C. John Colombos, *The International Law of the Sea* (3d rev. ed., London, Longmans, Green, 1954), p. 253. Cf. *The Scotia*, 14 Wall. 170 (1871).

A third method, namely the negotiation of international conventions, has also been used by the international maritime community, as for example in the Brussels conventions of 1910 "for the unification of certain rules of law in regard to collisions" and "for the unification of certain rules of law respecting assistance and salvage at sea."[79]

The maritime community was not satisfied with the rule of criminal jurisdiction laid down in 1927 by the Permanent Court of International Justice in *The Lotus* case. That decision upheld the right of Turkey to bring to trial in Turkey the commanding officer of a French ship which negligently collided with a Turkish ship on the high seas, resulting in the loss of Turkish lives. The League of Nations, the ILO, the International Maritime Committee, and others were induced to address themselves to the problem, with the result that an international convention was signed at Brussels in 1952 incorporating the rule that in such cases only the flag state would have jurisdiction in disciplinary or criminal proceedings.[80] The convention has not yet been generally ratified, but it affords a good example of the international parallel to national situations in which Congress is induced to enact new law when the old law, as interpreted by the Supreme Court, does not reflect the interests and desires of that part of the community particularly affected.

In the United States it has not been very difficult to secure action in the interests of uniformity with respect to mari-

79. Colombos, p. 258.
80. Philip C. Jessup, "The Growth of the Law," 29 *American Journal of International Law* 495 (1935); Colombos, pp. 228–32.

time law, because the Constitution extends the federal judicial power "to all cases of admiralty and maritime jurisdiction." It may be hard to imagine that the United States
would play a leading role in bringing about in broader fields
agreement on rules of transnational law which would be
applied in our forty-nine judicial jurisdictions. Long before
Mr. Bricker became the eponym of a new term for political
and constitutional provincialism, the United States Government declined to become a party to any of the general
treaties of private international law by which so many states
of the world are bound. A good omen is the strongly supported proposal for the establishment by Congress of a
Commission and Advisory Committee on International
Rules of Judicial Procedure which is to "investigate and study
existing practices of judicial assistance and coöperation between the United States and foreign countries with a view
to achieving improvements."[81] The facilities and resources
of the United Nations could be utilized for this purpose to
great advantage. Governments have been accustomed to
use international or transnational organizations for the solution of transnational problems. The experience is now of
respectable age in dealing with postal communications,
telecommunications, health, narcotics, fisheries, railways,
aviation, shipping, raw materials, labor, and many others.

81. The Attorney General's support for such legislation and other reasons
advanced for its passage are contained in H.R. Report no. 1363, 84th Congress, 1st Session, July 25, 1955, to accompany H.R. 7500. See Harry L.
Jones, "A Commission and Advisory Committee on International Rules
of Judicial Procedure," 49 *American Journal of International Law* 379 (1955).

They were not ready to accept the International Trade Organization under the Havana Charter, but a new attempt in the same field is being made through the United Nations Ad Hoc Committee on Restrictive Business Practices.[82] The State Department, however, opposed the adoption of the Committee's recommendations.[83] NATO has still to find an acceptable program for fulfilling the potentialities of Article 2 of the North Atlantic Treaty, but on a more restricted regional basis the European Coal and Steel Community has blazed a trail for supranational authorities.

Nevertheless, if there be any virtue in developing transnational law, much more exploration and analysis would need to precede the ponderous tread of governmental action. In the words of Mr. Justice Holmes: "The danger is that the able and practical minded should look with indifference or distrust upon ideas the connection of which with their business is remote."[84] So must the headlong scholar supply the proverbial characterization to himself where the foreign offices, the legislatures, and the courts still fear to tread. Seeing they themselves are wise, they may suffer the scholar gladly.

82. Cf. Dean Rostow's endorsement of such an international solution in his dissenting opinion (supported by Wendell Berge) in *Report of the Attorney General's National Committee to Study the Antitrust Laws* (1955), pp. 99, 102.

83. 32 *Department of State Bulletin* 665 (April 18, 1955).

84. Oliver Wendell Holmes, "The Path of the Law," *Collected Legal Papers* (New York, Harcourt, Brace, 1921), p. 201.

THE STORRS LECTURES

PUBLISHED BY THE YALE UNIVERSITY PRESS

(Volumes in print)

WESTMAR COLLEGE LIBRARY.